With the creativity of  insight into what life is read for everyone in C._____ you read it with your spouse, you will find that both your marriage and ministry will prosper. If you ignore this book now, you may find yourself picking it up a few years from now to discover why your marriage or ministry failed. Don't wait. Read it now.

JOE BEAM
Founder and Chairman, Family Dynamics

Few things in life are as destructive as infidelity on the part of a minister. Steve Hayes draws on his ministerial and counseling experience, guiding the reader on a journey into the heart of an all-too-common process. Ministers and spouses will greatly benefit from reading and discussing the material in *Safe & Sound*.

SCOTT FLOYD, PH.D.
Associate Professor of Counseling
Southwestern Baptist Theological Seminary

Steve Hayes has held up a mirror for every person desiring long-term effective ministry. This question is, "Can you handle the truth?" This book is full of truth!

DARIUS JOHNSTON
Senior Pastor
Christ Church Assembly of God
Fort Worth, Texas

I have had the privilege of reading the manuscript of Steve's new book, *Safe & Sound*. Having lived through much of what I read, the Lord so used this book to minister to me personally, and I believe he is doing the same to countless others who have walked through similar paths. As a former pastor's wife and now a single mother of four-plus years, I know firsthand the devastation that adultery can bring into a family. But I also know that the Lord is a God of restoration, and Steve's book beautifully points to the hope found in him. I only wish it had been written when my family's life was being turned upside down, but I am so thrilled to know of the precious ones who will benefit from its wisdom and insight. I highly recommend it to all who find themselves wondering where to turn. Jesus came to heal the brokenhearted and bind up their wounds, and my heart's desire is to see his people allow him to do just that. This book will point you in the right direction.

DAWN SMITH JORDAN
Singer/songwriter/recording artist, Urgent Records
Author, *Grace So Amazing*

This is a very clear, practical presentation of the subtle process of how temptation can come to ministers and their wives. Readers are drawn into the contemporary story and challenged to reflect on their own personal lives. This is recommended reading for all who want to protect themselves, their families, and their congregations from the tragic consequences of being blind to temptation.

REBEKAH R. LAND, PH.D
Family and Marriage Therapist
Nashville, Tennessee

This is a timely book that addresses what is becoming one of the great needs of the American church today. Rather than merely lament the situation, this tries to provide awareness of the Enemy's schemes and human weakness that lead to moral failure.

AL MEREDITH
Pastor, Wedgwood Baptist Church
Fort Worth, Texas

This book is both a word of warning and of grace. Using solid biblical reasoning and insightful analysis, Steve Hayes demonstrates how affairs in the ministry don't just happen but follow a predictable process. This book will be very helpful to the young pastor who is just beginning to understand the unique demands and temptations of the ministry. At the same time it is a wake-up call for the seasoned pastor who has danced too close to the edge of an affair. The comments regarding "the three laws of relationships" are worth the price of the book. They show convincingly why the promise will always exceed the reality of an affair. But there is also a word of grace—grace for those who struggle with temptation—and a glimpse of hope and redemption for the fallen.

DAVID A. MILLER
Senior Pastor
Faith Presbyterian Church
Seminole, Florida

Steve has written caringly and carefully on a timeless and timely topic, the integrity and fidelity of Christian marriage and ministry. *Safe & Sound* serves as a steadfast reminder and review-reference for the individual minister, as well as an inspirational textbook for ministry training.

Through the prism of my own marriage and ministry of more than fifty years, I view Steve's book to be relevant.

ROBERT H. SPEAR
Church of the Nazarene

Safe & Sound is a timely work written from the perspective of one who has helped many marriages through difficult times. Steve Hayes offers a creative and biblical approach to strengthening and healing ministry marriages. This book will be helpful to couples in ministry and to counselors.

FERN SUTTON
Counselor
Woodmont Hills Counseling Center
Nashville, Tennessee

JERRY SUTTON
Pastor, Two Rivers Baptist Church
Nashville, Tennessee

Title this book *A Course You Should Get in Seminary,* as pastor/counselor Steve Hayes honestly spills the dynamics of how pastors subtly fall to the attractive temptation of the extramarital affair. His parallel tracks of personal testimonies and biblical stories make for a scary but helpful treatment of how affairs sabotage a marriage and a ministry. The web of blame, sin, psychological needs, distractions, not paying attention to your spouse, discovering wandering thoughts and ready seducers gives Hayes the ammo to reveal with sobering bluntness a pattern that should scare all of us away from the lure of an affair. What is very risky and yet helpful is that Hayes goes out on a limb to provide one possibly helpful way for a church board to respond when a pastor succumbs. Not a fun read, but not discouraging either, here is wise help and a must read for returning street-smartness to fight an alarming pastoral trend.

TOM TYNDALL
Presbyterian pastor
Cofounder, Great Mates Ministries

Safe & Sound is long overdue. It is a must read for every couple in ministry. Chapter 6 is worth the price of the book. Husbands and wives are challenged to understand and identify the warning signals and biblically based principles to safeguard their marriages. Throughout this book, Steve Hays challenges Christian leaders to be accountable, to arm themselves to protect their marriages "from the grasp of temptations that could destroy their marriages." This book should be required reading for every seminary couple.

PATTI WEBB (MRS. HENRY)
Minister's wife
Coauthor, *A Mother's Garden of Prayer*
and *A Woman's Garden of Prayer*

SAFE & SOUND

SAFE & SOUND

Protecting *Personal* and *Ministry* Relationships

STEVE HAYES

FOREWORD BY ADRIAN ROGERS

BROADMAN
&HOLMAN
PUBLISHERS

Nashville, Tennessee

0–8054–2494–6

Published by Broadman & Holman Publishers
Nashville, Tennessee

Dewey Decimal Classification: 253
Subject Heading: MINISTERS / CHRISTIAN ETHICS

1 2 3 4 5 6 7 8 9 10 07 06 05 04 03 02

To my family for your love, patience, and sacrifice,
and most of all for believing in me

My darling wife, Kim
My precious children: Taylor, Graham, and Anna Spencer

*Trusting that God will see our family through
this journey safe and sound.*

Contents

Foreword

As ministers, we have all experienced the shock waves of moral failure among our ranks. Each of us wrestles with temptation to some degree. You may be experiencing your own struggle in this area or that of a fellow staff member. Nonetheless, we are fearful of dragging this issue of marital infidelity among ministers and their spouses out of the shadows and into the spotlight of the Holy Spirit. No longer do ministers have to ask the question, "How could this have happened?" *Safe & Sound* takes us inside the marriage, the mind, and the stresses of a minister sliding down the slippery slope of temptation.

After reading this book, you will be able to detect the warning signs of temptation much sooner, enabling you to take action to safeguard your marital and ministerial relationships.

I am impressed with the creative and insightful way that Steve Hayes expounds on James 1:13–16, revealing that an emotionally bankrupt marriage and moral failure is not an event, but a process. While the pages of this book are replete with Scripture references, *Safe & Sound* is not merely an expanded Bible study or sermon. These pages blend the insights of a counselor with the truth of God's Word, as gleaned by a husband and pastor.

No one ever arrives at a point in life or ministry beyond the reach of temptation. You will not have to seek out temptation—it will find you. It is my deepest desire that you will read this book and be prepared to respond properly to the temptations that are certain to come your way. Now is the time, *before* you think you need it.

After reading this book with yourself and your marriage in mind, share it with your staff, peers, or any group that you are mentoring for future ministry. You may choose to read it together as a group in order to strengthen your resolve to be above reproach and to develop a network of "lifeguards" to whom you are accountable.

I urge Christian educators to use this book as a tool to better prepare future generations of ministers to deal with this issue of moral wholeness. I commend to you *Safe & Sound* as an essential part of your curriculum.

Now, more than ever before, we as ministers must recommit to a life of personal integrity before a watching world. It is imperative that we further equip ourselves to be proactive in the area of marital faithfulness if we are to finish this race *Safe & Sound.*

—Adrian Rogers

PREFACE

Can You Handle the Truth?

"Do not think of yourself more highly than you ought, but rather think of yourself with sober judgment" (Rom. 12:3 NIV).

This is not a book for the proud, the superspiritual, or those too weak in character to be honest with themselves. The chapters that follow are for ministers who have the courage to tell the truth to themselves, God, and their spouses. These pages were written for Christian leaders who are willing to be accountable.

> The chapters that follow are for ministers who have the courage to tell the truth to themselves, God, and their spouses.

I assume that you have chosen this book because you and your spouse, or some couple you love deeply, have committed your future to career ministry. Our purpose is to focus on the marriages of ministers. The goal is to arm ministers and their spouses with the knowledge needed to elude the grasp of temptations that would destroy their marriage and their ministry. The reasons for and the sources from which this book has been written are pastoral, personal, and professional.

Since the age of seventeen, Christian ministry has shaped my life in some form or fashion as a volunteer, a student serving part-time on a church staff, and a full-time career minister. I have had fine acquaintances, friendships, and mentors from a varied landscape of ministry. Others who have affected my life are ministers whom I have never met, but whom I have admired from a distance. Memories of them bring great fondness of heart, but sadness as well, for many have been disqualified from ministry or suffered great setbacks because of moral failure or poor judgment. These words are written from a pastor's heart in an attempt to stem the tide of fellow ministers and congregational volunteers whose ministries are being cut short.

> I often think I would rather face the obvious manifestations of the demonic than the subtle persuasion of enticement.

The words on these pages are also written with a reverent fear of the Lord and a sobering respect for the power of temptation that arises out of personal experience. Like my brothers and sisters, I have also experienced the power of the enemy bearing down on my human and spiritual weaknesses. We do not have to pursue temptation; it will come looking for us.

Any minister who is determined to complete his journey with his marriage and ministry intact must examine himself, the spiritual realities with which he will have to contend, and the known challenges of his course.

Perhaps you've read a few books on Satan, demonic strongholds, bondage, and deliverance. *But how many books have you read on the process of temptation?* This is the battle most of us face from day to day. I often think I would rather face the obvious manifestations of the demonic than the subtle persuasion of enticement.

PREFACE: CAN YOU HANDLE THE TRUTH?

Have you ever wished you could get a look at Satan's playbook? Well, this is about as close as it gets. I hope you'll make the most of this opportunity. After several years of working with marriages in crises, I address this topic with insights gleaned from professional experience. Serving as a minister of counseling in the Christian community, I have been afforded a unique view into Christian marriages as they struggle with the temptation of moral failure.

Satan does not want you to read this book. Please pray for protection every time you pick it up and ask God to empower you to finish it. May God bless you, and may we all finish the journey with our marriages and ministries *Safe & Sound.*

—Steve Hayes

Acknowledgments

Thanks to my mom and dad, Speed and Bilye Hayes, for the foundation they've given me. Thank you to my in-laws, Aubrey and Anna House, for all of your support and for making your home available for me to escape and write.

To Becky Barnett and Melissa Wohlwend, thank you for your patience and persistence in walking with me through the creative process, for the encouragement and support, the prayers and long hours of work. I appreciate you more than you know.

Thank you, Len Goss and others at Broadman & Holman, for your faith that we could produce this book.

And thank you to friends who have shared their time and resources in making this book a reality: Kathy and Spence Lyon, Sandy Sanders, and Stephanie Mueller.

I appreciate my many peers—you know who you are—who have assisted me in the refining of my thoughts. You have helped shape the insights reflected in this book.

Prologue

Sam Bailey stepped into his office breathing a sigh of relief and rubbing the back of his neck in a futile attempt to relieve some of his tension. As he loosened his tie slightly and looked at his watch, he thought, *I wonder what I'll have to face when I get home. Will Angela still be up? I hope she's gone to bed. I can't handle another argument after a leadership meeting like the one I had tonight. I'm not sure who resents me the most, Mr. Torrence or my wife. They both seem to have my number these days.*

Suddenly sensing he was not alone, Sam looked over his left shoulder to see Karen standing in the door. In her usual soft-spoken manner, she said, "I came back to the conference room because I forgot my planner, and I noticed your light was on." Karen, always going the extra step, continued, "I thought you handled the meeting well this evening. The two ministers who preceded you were too intimidated to stand up to Mr. Torrence."

"Oh, I'm intimidated," Sam replied. "I just try not to let it show so I can keep the group focused on what needs to be done."

"You hide it well," she said with a smile. "Good night." And she left the office as quietly as she had appeared.

His headache seemed to pulse between his temples like a drum. Sam continued to pull his papers together and straighten his desk as jumbled thoughts raced through his mind: *My head is*

killing me! I've got to exercise more or do something to relieve this
stress; Angela is going to be so mad that I'm getting in this late again;
I bet Mr. Torrence is determined to have my resignation inside of six
months; I've got that funeral tomorrow; where are my notes? Karen
sure is sweet and it was nice to hear an encouraging word; I can't
believe her husband doesn't seem to appreciate what a blessing she is; she
is always so positive. I wish Angela would support me like that; tomor-
row is going to be a hard day; I had better get home; I hope Angela's
asleep so I can watch some TV and relax.

Sam looked over his desk one last time as he viewed the
notes, budget papers, and weekly bulletin. He decided to turn out
the light before he began to feel overwhelmed again. He turned
off his pager and cell phone, realizing he was looking forward to
a peaceful ride home.

Sam turned the key as he locked the door to his office with
one hand and held his briefcase in the other. He stepped out of
the church into the cool night air. Breathing deeply, Sam felt a
little more refreshed as the crisp air filled his lungs. Opening the
car door, he tossed his briefcase into the passenger seat, slid
behind the steering wheel, and then pulled the door closed.
Hearing the door seal shut, Sam paused before he started the
engine to relish the solace and the silence of his economy four-
door refuge.

With a sigh and a slight twist of the wrist, he turned the key,
and the starter strained but gave a fruitless effort. Sam turned the
key for a second attempt, and the engine roared to life. With a
smirk and a touch of humor in his voice, the grateful owner patted the dash and spoke a word of encouragement, "You got me
through seminary, darlin', and on my salary I can't afford for you

to give up on me now." Looking over his shoulder as he put his car in reverse, Sam made a mental note that once again his car was the only one left in the church parking lot, except for that old brown sedan that had been parked in the corner near the street for almost a week.

I need to remind Doris tomorrow that we need to do something about getting rid of that car. He sighed again. *That's all I need—one more thing.* The transmission clicked into drive, and he cut across the parking lot to the closest exit.

Nearing the end of his almost twenty-minute drive home, Sam pondered why the car stereo sounded so much better at night. He also noticed that the iridescent numbers on his dash and stereo made even this basic model seem high tech. As he turned on to his street and approached the driveway to his house, Sam felt the tension begin to build once again. He began rehearsing how he would respond if Angela were still up.

After a long day of chasing two-year-old Sara, forcing Jon to do his reading, assisting twelve-year-old Tommy with a last-minute school project, and baths and bedtime stories, Angela stood staring out the kitchen window. She was trying to summon the strength to clean the dishes from dinner and mentally take inventory of what the kids had to wear to school tomorrow. Her thoughts were interrupted abruptly when she noticed the headlights from Sam's car pulling into the drive. Resentment and other unnamed feelings filled Angela's heart until a lump settled in her throat. Suddenly, Sam was not the only one rehearsing what would be said when he walked through the door.

As Sam coasted down the driveway, he could see his wife's silhouette in the kitchen window. Immediately his neck stiffened, and his shoulders tightened as he prepared for the inevitable—another confrontation.

Angela listened as Sam's car pulled to a stop, idled for a moment, and then cut off. Tears settled in the rim of her eyes, and she quickly wiped them away as she heard the screen door slam shut and Sam's footsteps on the back porch. She replaced her feelings of rejection and hurt with anger and armed herself with words of sarcasm as the side door to the kitchen opened. "I'm glad you made it home so soon. Your timing is perfect. The kids are in bed, and Tommy's school project you had promised to help with is all done. It's not as good as you could have done, but it was the best we could do. We waited as long as we could."

Sam didn't even acknowledge her comment. He immediately took an aggressive and critical posture. "Well, you sure didn't spend your time keeping the house straight. Look at this place. What if someone from the church dropped by and saw what a mess this place is in? They might think that if we can't run our own household, we can't lead God's. We discussed keeping the main room of the house neat so . . ."

Angela interrupted, her voice escalating, "Well, then maybe they would be right. You're not running your household. I am. You're never here!"

Sam responded at a volume matching Angela's. "Is this the respect I get for the sacrifices I make for the kingdom of God and this family, so you can stay home with the children like we always dreamed?"

Sensing a quiver in her voice, Angela stopped. The silence was tense. In a quiet, intense whisper, she continued, "I didn't know staying home would mean becoming a single parent. I feel like the church is your wife, and I'm the mistress you have an occasional rendezvous with. . . . and Tommy . . . I think Tommy feels like the church has stolen his dad." She was no longer whispering, but she spoke in her usual voice, slowly, more thoughtfully, and more hopeless than before. "Do you know how many weekends have passed since you promised to take him fishing? I tried to be positive and give him the 'We have to share Daddy' speech. Then his reply just ripped my heart out: 'Mommy, how come we always have to share Daddy with the church, but the church never shares Daddy with us? He belonged to us first.'" She looked up at Sam with tears streaming down her face.

Sam, not knowing what to say, headed toward the bedroom murmuring, "I'm too tired to hash this out any further. I've got a headache. I'm going to take some medicine and lie down."

Frustrated, Angela turned back toward the kitchen sink as she picked up a now-cold dishcloth. She didn't even seem to notice its clammy feel as she stood there looking out the window with a blank stare. Her heart aching, she began to half cry and half pray: "Dear God, how did we get so messed up? Lord, I know Sam is working hard, and I know you have your hand on his life. But I'm losing sight of the godly young man who touched my heart and my soul. I can't seem to talk to him. When I hear him preach or see him come in late from visitation, I feel so neglected and betrayed. I know the ministry is not supposed to be easy, and I feel so guilty when I respond this way. I feel like the children and I are such a distant second place to the church, and when I think about it, I get so angry. Then I don't even want to be in the same room with Sam, much less have him touch me. We can't keep going on this way. Please help us!"

5

Sam walked into the master bathroom, opened the cabinet, took down a nearly empty bottle of headache medicine, and filled a cup with water. While the water was still running, he cupped his hands and splashed his face. He stared at himself in the mirror just long enough to see a look of disapproval. He threw his head back, swallowed a couple of pills, and then walked into the master bedroom where he collapsed on their queen-size bed. Lately, with growing distance between him and Angela, it had felt more like a king-size bed. Sam lay there staring at the ceiling fan as the swishing blades made a strobelike effect on the ceiling. While his mind was still racing with one thought after another, he began to half talk to himself and half pray: "God, what am I supposed to do? I've tried to tell her what it takes to succeed in the ministry, and she just doesn't seem to understand. It seems that every success at church is matched by even greater failure at home. Lord, you've got to get through to Angela. She needs to understand what the call to ministry is all about."

> It is expected of clergy to have an exemplary marriage and home life, yet the reality may be that their marriages are the most vulnerable of all.

Not waiting for the medicine to take effect, he drifted off to sleep.

The stress and the sentiments expressed by Sam and Angela are very real and commonplace. Pastors, staff, and clergy are privileged to be a part of one of the most rewarding of careers and yet one of the most overwhelming as well. The expectations are often unrealistic, and the scope of congregational needs is greater than any inexperienced pastor could ever anticipate. These dynamics are further complicated by the fact that ministers often have to perform in an environment where they feel misunderstood and unappreciated. After a while it seems as if someone always has an agenda or an axe to grind. If a young pastor underestimates the stress of the ministry, how much greater is the shock for his young wife?

It is expected of clergy to have an exemplary marriage and home life, yet the reality may be that their marriages are the most vulnerable of all. If we look closely at Sam's marriage and ministry, we easily see that he has a lot working against him. *If he fails to realize the severity of his eroding relationship with his wife, the significance of his growing emotional neediness, and his inability to manage stress, he will soon become a casualty of ministry.* He will be the subject of "what a pity" conversations among his peers as they discuss the news of his sudden resignation. Then they will probably change the subject before they are forced to consider the implications this might have for their own lives.

We must ask God for the motivation to take a courageous look at the difficult realities claiming an ever increasing number of ministries and marriages among the Lord's anointed. I pray that these pages will equip pastors and their spouses to protect the integrity of their relationships. It is also the desire of my heart that churches use this book as an inspiration to become proactive in developing policies and strategies to protect and respond properly to ministers when they struggle. Ministers and their spouses need safety and support from the church when they are being tempted and tested.

Note: The author recognizes that in an increasing number of marriages, the husband is not the one in the official ministry position. I ask that if this is your situation, read with understanding rather than take offense.

CHAPTER 1

God's Calling

It was a new day, and Sam found himself sitting in his office with his Bible in his lap. He was the only one in the office, but this moment was anything but peaceful or relaxing. He kept repeating his thoughts to himself in an arduous cycle as he reviewed the unresolved conflict with his wife the night before. He tried to read his Bible, but he was too distracted. He tried to pray, but his mind repeatedly replayed their argument.

The residual tension between him and Angela during breakfast had left each of them feeling isolated and distant. Sam had finally broken the silence by offering to take Tommy to school so he would not have to take his school project on the bus. He remembered the way Tommy's face seemed to light up at the suggestion. Taking his son to school and helping him set up his project had been the only redeeming aspect of the morning.

Frustrated, a cry from his heart escaped his lips, "Why, God? Why does life have to be so hard? Is this the cost of ministry? Are Angela's expectations too high? Is it me? What can I do? Am I really neglecting my family? Why did you call me to *this?* This is not at all what I thought the ministry would be like. I'm not happy, my family is not happy, and the church doesn't seem too happy either!" As the words tumbled out, he was at once angry and discouraged. "Is this why I pushed myself to get through seminary? Is this all there is?"

Sam's eyes fell to the page where his Bible lay open in his lap. There it was, jumping off the page in red letters. The answer of a young adolescent boy responding to his anxious parents: "Did you not know that I must be about My Father's business?" (Luke 2:49).

Such clarity of mission and resolute confidence in a heavenly calling coming from the lips of a twelve-year-old boy was astounding. Sam began to ponder the verse's meaning. *I know this was Jesus, but could I be equally as certain of your direction for my life?*

The thoughtful prayer became audible: "I used to be so certain. I was so excited and grateful when you saved me and changed my life. Could it be that *I* presumed I should become a preacher, and you never intended this for me at all?"

The thoughts continued pouring out as he began conversing more with himself than with God. *My family has never known God, and he has done so much to improve my marriage. I owed God a tremendous debt. Angela wasn't so sure about the ministry at first, but she came around. . . . Did I pressure her into changing her mind? It was difficult, but Angela seemed to like our life at seminary. At times, though, I wondered if I had made the right decision. I wasn't sure I had what it took. I think I would have quit, but I had brought my family halfway across the country, and our home church was so proud. They sent us money every month. How could I ever admit that it might be a mistake? No, I couldn't let them down—all those people who believed in me. But the real question is:* Did I hear you? *Or was I just "sticking it out" for all the wrong reasons?*

EXAMINE YOURSELVES TO MAKE SURE

Did Sam enter the ministry because of God's call, or did he somehow manufacture a call of his own? Did he mistake the blessing of God's grace for the call to ministry? This is, of course, a personal issue between Sam and God. The odds are he may very well have heard God's call correctly, but his confidence was shaken. His ability to properly love his wife and her ability to give him the support he needs are very limited. It is likely that Sam's ministry is being hindered by his lack of oneness with his wife.

What about you? Have you ever questioned God's call on your life after committing to the ministry? Questioning is not necessarily a sign of a misguided calling. Questioning one's usefulness for God's purpose may actually be a sign that you are truly called. This would place you in the company of many of God's greatest servants. Consider Moses, who, after a burning-bush experience, a conversation with God, three miracles, and the promise of God's presence, still incited God's wrath because he felt so handicapped and afraid. God had to enlist Aaron for additional support (see Exod. 3–4).

Then there was Elijah, who ran from the death threat of Jezebel. In his exhaustion and shame, he asked God to kill him, saying, "I am no better than my fathers!" (1 Kings 19:4). This was the man who called down fire from heaven and led the wayward nation of Israel to purge their land of 850 prophets of Baal and Asherah. It was a great day for Israel, and Elijah was God's man.

However, Elijah was weak and tired and stressed from the great ordeal when Jezebel blindsided him with her venomous note. It is common for men struggling with the stress of ministry to be blindsided and to doubt their usefulness to God. Praise God that he is gracious and patient. Sensing Moses' need for additional support, he provided Aaron, and sensing Elijah's exhaustion, God sent an angel to bring him nourishment.

> God would rather we ask questions and allow him to reassure or redirect us than for us to wander in disillusionment.

God is loving enough and big enough for us to question him. God would rather we ask questions and allow him to reassure or redirect us than for us to wander in disillusionment. We must not be afraid to be honest with God or ourselves. We have to be certain of God's call because we will have days, maybe months, maybe even years, when his call will be all we have to hang on to.

SOME PREACH BECAUSE OF SELFISH AMBITION AND SOME BECAUSE OF GOODWILL

It is amazing how the call to ministry can rearrange a person's life. When I was attending seminary, I often found that the classmate in the desk next to me might be a gentleman fifteen years my senior. Unlike me, he obviously did not take a direct path from college to graduate school. He was a seasoned adult with a family and had given up a nice house with a pool, expensive cars, and a successful career. He uprooted his family to live in an apartment and work odd jobs. He would have to spend longer hours in the library in an attempt to relearn the art of being a successful student.

When other men faced their midlife years by deserting their families for younger women and faster cars, these men loaded themselves and their wives into a rented truck and sold their homes. What would possess a man and his gracious wife to do such a thing? If you asked them, they would not refer to this bizarre behavior as a midlife crisis but rather a midlife calling. I always felt a little unworthy to be sitting next to a man who had joyfully made such sacrifices.

However, not every student who sat next to me in pursuit of a divinity degree was so noble of character or a worthy model of faith and spiritual maturity. In fact, it often seemed quite the opposite. While these men and women also claimed to be called of God, many would never finish the degree program, or they would be disqualified from ministry within a few years after graduation. Their ministry would be ruined by failed marriages, adulterous affairs, addictive behaviors, and other immoral behaviors unbecoming a minister.

Other peers, who bore the fruit of a true call from God, would become severely wounded when called by churches to work with ministers who seemed incapable of displaying the grace of our Lord. These church leaders often turned out to be controlling, deceitful, manipulative, and insecure people who lacked integrity. Sadly, they somehow had managed to work their way into influential positions of ministry.

The New Testament seems to reveal at least four different profiles of ministers. The apostle Paul made note of this great discrepancy among men who were preaching the gospel. In Philippians 1:15, Paul spoke of two types of ministers: some who *preached Christ out of envy and strife* while others *preached Christ out of goodwill.* The apostle Paul in his second letter to Timothy warned of false teachers and prophets who served only their appetites while leading others astray. In his second epistle, the apostle Peter included a similar warning.

In Acts 15:37–40, we read about "John called Mark," who represents a *third profile for a minister.* Paul became very disenchanted with Mark when he failed to complete their missionary journey. Thanks to Barnabas, Mark was later restored to ministry. *Mark represents a man genuinely called of God who embarks enthusiastically on ministry before he is ready.* For those who fall into this pattern, the pressures of ministry will expose their greatest weaknesses and plunge them into failure unless some type of support and accountability system is established.

> The ministry is too stressful and the temptations that come are too great for a minister and his family to be uncertain of God's calling.

This may have been the case of several of my seminary peers who disqualified themselves so early in the race. They embarked on their ministries before fully addressing the weaknesses in their character or unmanageable behaviors.

In 1 Timothy, we read about *the fourth profile for a minister.* This profile should encourage any minister to take a sobering look in the mirror. *This is the minister who, no matter how clear his call, his success in ministry, or his diligent preparation, can still become disqualified because of the weaknesses of the flesh and therefore must never underestimate the subtlety of temptation.* Paul admonished Timothy to be an example in word, conduct, love, spirit, faith, purity, and doctrine (1 Tim. 4:11–15).

Then in verse 16, he writes, "*Take heed to yourself* and to the doctrine. Continue in them, for in doing this you will save both yourself and those who hear you" (emphasis added).

Some of the greatest orators and some of the most innovative, creative, and successful ministers I've known have been able to perform in their ministries while at the same time participating in some of the most defiling of sins. I realize God does not grade sin, because it is all death, but some sins violate, use, and disgrace a greater number of people than other sins. When these great leaders were finally exposed, their fall was disastrous for their families and the reputation of the church.

Consequently, it is imperative that if we are going to finish the race safe and sound, with our ministries intact, we *must know* that God's call rests on our lives. We must also be certain that our wives and families are as equally convinced and committed to God's claim on our future. The ministry is too stressful and the temptations that come are too great for a minister and his family to be uncertain of God's calling. If a couple is not completely and evenly yoked in their commitment to God's call, I advise them to wait until they are. For if a couple is not completely united, Satan will find the place of division, and he will wedge the two apart and then devour their relationship and their ministry.

"What Pastors' Wives Wish Their Churches Knew, Part 2" was an article in the April 1997 edition of *Christianity Today*. The article acknowledged this shocking realization as the author quoted syndicated columnist Terry Mattingly: "The divorce rate for U.S. pastors rose sixty-five percent in the past twenty-five years. Eighty percent said their ministry has 'a negative impact' on their home life, while one-third said the pastorate has been a 'hazard' to their families." If we are going to maintain the passion in our marriage and our ministry, we must be equally committed and undeniably convinced of God's call on our lives. There is no other way.

God's Calling

Abraham

"Now the LORD had said to Abram: 'Get out of your country, from your family and from your father's house, to a land that I will show you'" (Gen. 12:1).

Jacob

"And behold, the LORD stood above it and said: 'I am the LORD God of Abraham your father and the God of Isaac; the land on which you lie I will give to you and your descendants. . . . Behold, I am with you and will keep you wherever you go'" (Gen. 28:13–15).

Isaiah

"Also I heard the voice of the LORD, saying: 'Whom shall I send, and who will go for Us?' Then I said, 'Here am I! Send me'" (Isa. 6:8).

Paul

"But when it pleased God, who separated me from my mother's womb and called me through His grace, to reveal His Son in me, that I might preach . . . ." (Gal. 1:15–16).

Timothy

"This charge I commit to you, son Timothy, according to the prophecies previously made concerning you, that by them you may wage the good warfare, having faith and a good conscience. . . ." (1 Tim. 1:18–19).

Pillar Page

In Genesis 28:12–19, God appeared to Jacob and spoke to him in a dream. The next day the Scripture says Jacob responded in the following manner: "Then Jacob rose early . . . took the stone . . . set it up as a pillar, and poured oil on top of it. . . . he called . . . that place Bethel . . . [house of God]."

Prayer: "Lord, open my eyes and speak to me, please, just as you did with Jacob. Amen."

In the Old Testament, God taught his people to set up markers to remind them of special times when God spoke to them or intervened on their behalf. This is the purpose of the Pillar Page throughout this book. Each pillar contains questions for the purpose of helping you ponder how the message of each chapter may be applied on a personal level. (If you are a person who likes to write, you may want to purchase a journal to accompany your journey through this book.)

- ❏ Describe your thoughts, your feelings, the time in your life when God revealed his Son in you (when you accepted Christ personally to be your Savior).
- ❏ Describe how you realized God was calling you, setting you apart for the purpose of full-time vocational ministry.
- ❏ In what ways were you personally aware that God had spoken to you concerning the ministry?
- ❏ In what ways did God confirm your call through others in the church out of which you were called?
- ❏ Was there a mentor who also confirmed your call like Paul did for Timothy?

❏ In what other ways has God continued to confirm his call on your life (opportunities for ministry, ways you sense God's pleasure as you minister, ways God has displayed his power when you minister)?

❏ Did your spouse agree to enter the ministry with you out of personal conviction from her own heart, or did she agree to follow you out of concession? How did God speak to your spouse?

❏ In what ways is your spouse equally fulfilled by sharing in the ministry? What excites your spouse the most about the privilege of your family being set aside for ministry?

If you find these questions difficult to answer, you may wish to seek counsel about God's direction for your life. The ministry, by nature, is stressful, and a person should not embark on such an overwhelming course with internal conflict or a divided home. If you are an experienced pastor who finds yourself dealing with these issues, you may need to consider a leave of absence, sabbatical and/or professional counseling to strengthen your marriage and unite your family. If these foundation issues are not resolved, it will greatly increase your susceptibility to temptation and failure. Your calling may be genuine, but some healing must take place before you can continue further.

CHAPTER 2

The Truth about the Tempter

Loner leaned back on his leathery wings as he rubbed his chin carefully to keep from scratching his distorted face with his long nails. *They're just about ready,* he thought to himself. As he listened to their argument in the kitchen, he could see that it was time for some assistance from a few of his associates. Loner, a demon of rejection, had been at work in the lives of Sam and Angela for years. Loner had been responsible for Sam's family, and his cousin, Loser, had been at work in Angela's family. When Sam and Angela were married, Loner stayed to work on the destruction of their relationship. Loser was reassigned to Angela's sister.

When Loner saw that Sam had gone to bed alone and that Angela was in tears at the kitchen window, he impressed even himself. Sensing he had done a good night's work, he left to report to Legion. He knew he would need the assistance of Bitterness, Lust, and Covetousness. Loner hated to ask for their assistance because they always tried to take all the credit. He preferred to work alone, of course, but he needed the others to complete the assignment.

Loner figured if he could assign Lust and Covetousness to Sam, then he and Bitterness could work on Angela. It was perfect—they only had to tolerate one another when Sam and Angela were both at home, and that was becoming less and less frequent.

Loner began to fill with fiendish pride as he flew to report to Legion. It was a strategy that had proven effective time and time again. He and Bitterness would cause Angela to keep pushing Sam away. She was becoming more and more convinced that Sam didn't really love her. She believed that he needed her just so he could stay in the ministry. Loner had fed her this lie less than a year into the ministry, and she had owned the idea as though it originated with her.

Lust and Covetousness would take advantage of Sam's loneliness and need for encouragement. Loner thought to himself, *God was a fool to create man with needs that are so easy to exploit! At just the right time, Karen will speak a positive word to Sam, and then Lust and Covetousness will go to work. This marriage will be in shambles in no time.* Loner was jolted out of his wicked imagination by the chill of evil that emanated from Legion's lair.

> Satan is not just a liar; he is the master of lies. He does not merely tell an untruth or misrepresent the facts. He creates a completely false view of reality.

(While this may be an imaginative approach, the spiritual realities addressed here are a very real danger. If a minister's calling and marriage are not secure and unified, Satan will divide and destroy. This is exactly what is taking place in Sam and Angela's relationship.)

The Great Deceiver

Satan is truly the great deceiver. The deadliest aspect of our archenemy is not that he is so powerful, overwhelming, or intimidating. It is not the threat of demon possession, disease, or even death. *It is his ability to deceive.*

This is why, in John 8:44, Jesus stated that the devil has been a liar from the very beginning and that he is the father of lies. Satan is not just a liar; he is the master of lies. He does not merely tell an untruth or misrepresent the facts. He creates a completely false view of reality. Throughout the Scriptures, Satan demonstrates that he is cunning and calculated.

We often experience evil as chaotic, random, and unpredictable. Yet Satan, the mastermind behind all sin, is always intelligent—not wise, but intelligent. In Ephesians 6:11–12, the devil is described as one who schemes, and his spiritual forces are listed in ranking order: principalities, then powers, then rulers, then spiritual hosts. The Gospel account where Jesus faces the demon named Legion implies that the forces of evil are organized and working in coordination with one another: "My name is Legion [a term for a Roman military unit]; for we are many" (Mark 5:9). Daniel 10:12–14 refers to the prince of Persia resisting God's angel who was attempting to deliver an interpretation to Daniel, revealing to us that the forces of darkness are assigned to regions or countries to thwart the work of God.

> The Gospel account where Jesus faces the demon named Legion implies that the forces of evil are organized and working in coordination with one another.

THIS WAR IS PERSONAL

Seemingly, Satan has his demons assigned to thwart the work of God in the lives of individuals as well. I don't believe it was merely a matter of circumstance that Satan addressed Eve instead of Adam. It is quite possible that Satan studied Adam and then studied Eve. He listened to their conversations and observed how the couple interacted with each other. He had surmised that Eve was more vulnerable to his deceptions. Perhaps Adam had a tendency to follow when he should have led. The serpent may have concluded that if he could get Eve to sin, then Adam would probably follow.

In Genesis 4:7, God has a conversation with the next generation when he issues a warning to Cain before he commits the sin of murder. In this conversation, God describes sin in terms of a personality who is waiting, observing, and preparing to pounce like a tiger on an unsuspecting prey. God was warning Cain that more is involved than the mere emotion of anger.

> The spiritual personality behind sin, whether it was Satan or a demon, was observing, making notes, and scheming.

What was sin waiting for? I'm convinced sin was watching, studying, and calculating when the moment would be right. The spiritual personality behind sin, whether it was Satan or a demon, was observing, making notes, and scheming. Sin studied the relationship between Cain and Abel in Genesis 4, just as the serpent studied the relationship between Adam and Eve in Genesis 3.

Sin noted every curt response, every argument, each resentful glance, the increasing acts of aggression, and finally, a resistance to God—the unwillingness to heed God's warning. Sin could observe the storm brewing inside Cain by his words and actions toward his brother. It was only a matter of time until the circumstances of Cain's life would align with the climate of his heart.

Like the clouds of a tropical storm waiting to circulate into a hurricane, so was Cain's heart waiting to unleash its storm of resentment, anger, and violence.

> Neither discipline in spiritual exercise, accumulated knowledge of Scripture, nor religious activity and accomplishments are accurate indicators of a person's heart. *The true indicator is relationships.*

Sin was anticipating the time when Cain would be blinded by his resentment and mastered by his anger. He would be completely deceived by the lie that his problem was Abel instead of his own wayward heart. Then all sin would need was the right opportunity. It is obvious that Satan can learn all he needs to know about us by watching our relationships with those who are closest to us. Just as Satan sold Cain the lie that Abel was his problem, he tries to convince us that our spouses are the source of our problems. This deception leads us to focus on changing our spouses instead of our own wayward hearts.

Relationships: Window to the Heart

Neither discipline in spiritual exercise, accumulated knowledge of Scripture, nor religious activity and accomplishments are accurate indicators of a person's heart. *The true indicator is relationships.* The way we respond to those who are the closest to us is the true indicator of the condition of the human heart. The apostle Paul in his treatise on love in 1 Corinthians 13 made this perfectly clear. He made it clear that spiritual giftedness and service were hollow and meaningless without love expressed in relationships.

The apostle John wrote in 1 John 1:7, "But if we walk in the light as He is in the light, we have fellowship with one another," making our relationships the measure of our spiritual health. John further wrote in 1 John 2:10, "He who loves his brother abides in the light, and there is no cause for stumbling in him." Peter wrote in 1 Peter 3:7, ". . . giving honor to the wife . . . as being heirs together of the grace of life." Then would it not be a logical conclusion that the health of our marriages and the way we respond to our spouses is the first and greatest test of our walk with Christ?

> Then would it not be a logical conclusion that the health of our marriages and the way we respond to our spouses will be the first and greatest test of our walk with Christ?

All Satan has to do to know how to subvert God's work in our lives is to watch our relationships. The look in our eyes, the words we choose, the tone of our voices, what we do or don't do, the emotions we share or withhold when we are with our spouses—these tell our enemy much of what he needs to know about us. By this, Satan identifies what needs are being met and what needs are being neglected. He is then able to use the information gathered to scheme and plan the destruction of our marriages and our ministries.

What can we conclude about Satan's mode of operation when he is at work in the lives of God's children?

- He is cunning, intelligent, and scheming.
- He is organized and has demonic forces assigned to thwart God's work in the lives of people as well as nations.
- Satan and those under him observe, study, and make note

of our habits, our tendencies, our weaknesses, and our strengths.

- Satan gains an understanding of the extent to which our hearts are unguarded by watching our eyes, listening to our words, and noting what we do and don't do.
- Our hearts become unguarded when we accept as truth the lies that Satan has subtly suggested to our hearts and minds over time.
- The best indicator of our relationship to God is how we treat those who are closest to us.
- Satan knows that his lies have taken root when we begin to mistreat our loved ones, grow distant, and resist God's truth or prompting.
- The forces of sin are patient. They are willing to wait for the most opportune moment.

THE TRUTH ABOUT THE TEMPTER

"Now the serpent was more cunning than any. . . . The woman said, 'The serpent deceived. . .'" (Gen. 3:1, 13).

"And do not lead us into temptation, but deliver us from the evil one" (Matt. 6:13).

"Now when the devil had ended every temptation, he departed from [Jesus] until an opportune time" (Luke 4:13).

"And the Lord said, 'Simon, Simon! Indeed, Satan has asked for you, that he may sift you as wheat. But I have prayed for you, that your faith should not fail'" (Luke 22:31–32a).

"Put on the whole armor of God, that you may be able to stand against the wiles [schemes] of the devil. For we do not wrestle against flesh and blood" (Eph. 6:11–12a).

Pillar Page

Prayer: "Lord, open my eyes and speak to me, please, just as you did with Jacob. Amen."

❏ When you think about your spouse, what feelings do you experience? Circle the items below that apply:

acceptance	safety	trust	respect
admiration	gratitude	sense of belonging	
attraction	contentment	a sense of closeness	
thankfulness	rejection	loneliness	
anger	distrust	disappointment	
insecurity	fear	resentment	

❏ Do you think these feelings are mutual?

❏ When you and your spouse interact, how do you respond to each other? You may consider answering by choosing one of the following for each question below:

Almost never   Seldom   Occasionally   Often

- Do the two of you look forward to the times you can spend together?
- Do you touch?
- Do you kiss?
- Do you hug?
- Are you respectful, gracious, and loving in the way you speak to each other?
- Do you gladly serve each other?
- Do you pray for each other?
- Do you spend time with God as a couple apart from church?
- Do you encourage each other?

- Do you honor each other?
- Do you share thoughts and feelings without wounding each other?
- Are the concerns and interests of each of you equally valued?
- Do you enjoy being together sexually and emotionally?
- Are you critical of each other?
- Is either of you easily angered?
- Do you feel the two of you are honest and open about your feelings and activities, or is there emotional distance and secrecy?
- Does either of you feel controlled, dominated, or unheard?
- Does either of you keep your thoughts to yourself because it is not worth the battle if you speak freely?
- Does either of you have difficulty expressing or receiving affection?
- Does either of you have any destructive habits such as pornography, drugs, alcohol, sexual addiction, gambling, sexual avoidance, physical or verbal abuse, etc.?
- Are there any mental health issues that may be unidentified or untreated? (Examples: depression, anxiety, obsessive compulsive behavior, eating disorders, other _____)

❏ Based on your answers, how would you describe the *unity* and *satisfaction* in your marriage? (Circle your answer.)

Excellent   Above average   Average   Marginal
Disappointed   Dissatisfied   Miserable

❏ Based on this assessment, how difficult do you think it would be for Satan to *sabotage* your marriage? (Circle your answer.)

Extremely challenging   Challenging
Difficult   Marginal
Fairly easy   Easy   "Walk-in-the-park"

❏ Based on the ratings above, *what commitment are you willing to make to God to strengthen your marriage?* (Check all that apply.)

   ❏ Continue to improve what you are already doing
   ❏ Commit to one-on-one time on a daily or almost daily basis
   ❏ Go on regular dates
   ❏ Humble yourself and seek forgiveness
   ❏ Make a concerted effort to encourage honest, open, and safe sharing of feelings, ideas, dreams, expectations, and disappointments
   ❏ Seek counseling

Special Note to Both Pastor and Spouse

If this questionnaire confirms that your marriage is in a bad place, then being in the ministry may put the two of you in a difficult position. On the one hand, there is obvious need for assistance, and on the other hand the church may misinterpret your efforts in seeking support.

This is a risk that may have to be taken to be proactive in your marriage. Ministers have taken different approaches to this issue. Some pastors go to a professional in another town to maintain anonymity, while other pastors inform the appropriate church leadership from the start.

A pastor may be able to separate his personal life by going to counseling in another town, but it has always amazed me how people still manage to talk. When a pastor is open with his leadership, then he controls the "press release," and he can enlist his leadership in handling the rumor mill.

A sample statement to leadership might be as follows: "As the trusted leadership in our church, I want you to be informed. My wife and I have a sound marriage, but we would like to fine-tune our relationship. So we will be going to see a counselor for several sessions. If you hear rumors of any other nature, I would appreciate your correcting any misinformation. I appreciate your support."

Chapter 3

Prelude to the Present

Each passing day the stress at the church continued to increase while attendance and offerings decreased. New jobs and newer homes had come to several towns only a forty-minute drive from Sam's community. Many of the key families in the church tried to make the commute, but after several months they decided to move.

Now I know what Paul meant about being poured out like a drink offering, Sam thought to himself while waiting for the light to change. *I continue to pour more and more of myself into this church, but no matter how hard I try, Mr. Torrence and his cronies become increasingly critical.*

The light changed and Sam proceeded with the flow of traffic, appearing entranced as he continued to ponder his situation. *It's not much better at home. The sacrifices I make for the Lord's work and for our family don't seem to score with Angela either. It's like she doesn't respect me anymore. She's showing less and less interest in what I do, and she's coming up with more and more excuses not to be involved at church. It's like we don't have anything in common any more except the kids.*

How did it all change so fast? We were such a team in seminary. It was the happiest we have ever been . . . I think. Why is everything so different now? It's like we don't even know each other. We can't agree on anything. What's missing? We're intelligent people; why can't we communicate? Why can't we connect anymore?

I wonder if she's considered giving up on us. She sure isn't happy. How could she do that to me? She wouldn't do that to the kids, but it's not like it hasn't happened before . . . I can't think this way . . .

When I get to the hospital, I'm going to get my own room. I could use a few days of R & R, an inclined bed, a television with a working remote, and a prepared meal . . . well, maybe I'm not that desperate yet. Sam awakened to consciousness as he approached the entrance to the hospital.

Angela sat on the park bench enjoying the warmth of the sun on her skin and the cool nip in the air that hinted fall wasn't far off. It was a beautifully refreshing day. The weather was perfect for watching the kids play in the park. But the climate inside Angela's heart wasn't quite so pleasant. She had gone to the park in an attempt to get over her frustration with Sam.

How could I have so misjudged him? she thought. *When we dated, he always made time for me. Then it seemed as if work was more important. But after he accepted Christ and we got active in church, it was better. When we went to seminary, the school hours were long, but we managed to make the most of his study breaks. We would have picnics on campus in the spring and watch the squirrels. In the fall we would get grocery sacks and the kids would run around campus picking up pecans while Sam and I walked around holding hands! Oh, and church—church was great! The people were so loving with lots of activities for the children. Sam was able to gain experience assisting the pastor, and we both helped with the youth occasionally.*

I miss those times of walking together. Almost every evening we found time for short walks when we would talk about our day and pray together. I can't remember the last time we really took time to pray together. I really miss it.

Why is it so different now? The children and I often eat dinner alone, or Sam rushes through the meal to get prepared for a committee meeting. It almost feels like Sam has exchanged the restaurant he used to manage for the church, and somehow I'm . . . no, the kids and I . . . are left out in the cold.

Well, if he thinks I'm going to be his quiet little pastor's wife who sits smiling on the front pew with her little ducklings in a row, he's got another thought coming. I've never let any man treat me like an afterthought. We're going to . . . Angela's thoughts were abruptly interrupted by Jon's scream as he tried to wipe the sand from his eyes.

CHILDHOOD INFLUENCES ADULTHOOD

Sam and Angela wondered how they could have misjudged each other. Sam didn't understand why he couldn't seem to reach her, and Angela couldn't understand why she never felt "good enough." It seems they used to speak the same language, but now they never seem to have anything in common. It's as if they are trying to decipher a secret code, but key pieces of information are missing.

> It's as if they are trying to decipher a secret code, but key pieces of information are missing.

Where can Sam and Angela find the missing pieces of information they so desperately need? Perhaps the understanding they need would be more easily identified by exploring their pasts instead of wrestling with the present. Often one can underestimate or fail to consider the influence our childhood has on our adulthood. That is not to say that we should escape the responsibility of the present by blaming the past. Yet it is important to remember that we are the most impressionable in our childhood and early teen years.

Our growing-up years are the years when we form our perceptions of the world and how it works. We learn what others expect of us and what we can expect from others. We make conclusions based on our experience about how we can get our needs met and care for the ones we love with the least amount of pain. Perhaps this is why Jesus said that those who would see the kingdom of heaven must become like little children (see Matt. 18:2–5). He understood that if the disciples were going to follow him, they would have to be open and allow God to rewrite the script by which they understood reality.

Sam and Angela are no different. The formula they are using to decipher the secret code of their relationship has missing pieces, and also distorted pieces. During their separate journeys through childhood, they each had essential needs that went unmet, which created deep longings, residual pain, and disheartening disappointments. Consequently, they developed unhealthy ways of managing relationships. They emerged from childhood with deep-seated feelings of disappointment in themselves as individuals. What they had learned about the people who were supposed to love them left Sam sensing he always had to work harder and Angela feeling that she wasn't good enough to be first on anyone's list.

Sam's dad was an alcoholic. When he was nine years old, his mom gave up and left. Sam got little acknowledgment from his father, but he still worked hard, and his excellent grades gained attention and praise from encouraging teachers.

Sam's interest in girls increased as he matured into his teen years. He was confident in his ability to succeed at school and work, but he felt awkward around girls. He couldn't talk to his dad about how he felt, and at times he really wished he had a mom around. He hadn't heard from her for a long time, so he avoided those feelings by convincing himself he didn't need her.

When Sam did give relationships a try, they didn't last very long. He would get very jealous and possessive. If Sam felt the girl he was dating might be having second thoughts about the relationship, he would break it off first. Then he would turn his attention back to work and school, pretending he didn't have time for girls.

Angela grew up in a Christian family that attended church on a fairly regular basis. Her mom and dad seemed to get along for the most part, but each one did their own thing. Her dad often traveled out of town on business, and he was always exhausted when he came home. However, he still managed to be very demanding at times. Although he occasionally said the words she longed to hear, something in how he said it created a sense of disapproval. It seemed he always wanted something from her—a certain behavior—more than he wanted her, his little girl.

Angela wanted nothing more than for her daddy to be with her and play with her, but he rarely did. She actually felt more comfortable when he was out of town. When she became a teenager, Angela and her dad had brutal arguments, and her mom was caught in the middle as a mediator. Since her dad rarely seemed to have time or energy for her, she resented any attempts he made as a parent to guide her. She developed a sharp tongue, and she could point out every mistake he ever made as a parent to get him to back off.

When Angela met Sam, he seemed to give her the attention she had always craved. He gave her little gifts, called her at different times throughout the day, and often traded shifts at work just to be with her. However, she didn't realize how superficial all of this was because she never developed an intimate relationship with her dad. In fact, the experience of true intimacy is one of the key pieces of information that Sam and Angela need in order to decipher the secret code of their relationship.

Sam seemed to have a mature attitude about life, and he was a hard worker. He also made Angela feel special. But after they were married, he stopped choosing her over work. Soon Angela realized she wasn't going to get much more attention from Sam than she did from her father. *He's just like my dad! I guess all men are alike!* she thought to herself (and sometimes yelled at Sam).

Hurt and resentful, Angela would often express her pain in the form of criticism and biting sarcasm. These were techniques she had mastered as a teenager when arguing with her dad. Reacting in this way often led to a heated battle of words, but she would at least have Sam's undivided attention. When Sam lost interest and turned away in silence, however, her sense of rejection and failure became almost unbearable.

Missing Pieces

My wife and I share the duty of taking our children to dental and medical appointments. One day while sitting in a waiting room, I looked up from a magazine to notice my daughter displaying frustration at the children's table covered with age-appropriate activities. I got out of my seat, walked across the room, and knelt down at her side to determine the source of her consternation. She was attempting to work a puzzle that had missing pieces. She had even been so resourceful as to collect pieces from another puzzle that had a similar design, but the pieces were not interchangeable because they were not cut exactly the same.

> **During our childhood and teen years, we gather pieces of information about ourselves, family, relationships, the world, and God.**

During our childhood and teen years, we gather pieces of information about ourselves, family, relationships, the world, and God. Throughout the years as we mature, we begin trying to put these pieces together to form a pattern that makes sense. The better the pieces fit together, the more secure and confident we feel. We develop a sense of safety, personal value, and control.

When we reach our teen years and young adulthood, we not only try to fit the pieces together but we start forming a picture of how life and love should be. It is similar to a completed jigsaw puzzle that forms a beautiful picture when all the pieces are in place.

I'm always amazed when I walk into someone's home and notice a beautifully framed picture that, upon closer inspection, turns out to be a puzzle. These pictures are made of thousands of uniquely cut pieces put together over a considerable amount of time. I'm amazed because I don't have the patience for such a project; if I find the patience, I almost always have a missing or damaged puzzle piece (or two) that makes the picture incomplete.

Sadly many of us find that we can't complete our emotional puzzle because essential pieces are missing or damaged and they don't fit. Pieces like acceptance, safety, security, respect, proper affection, genuine concern, confidence, and commitment are missing or distorted. Then, like my daughter trying to complete her puzzle, our hearts fill with frustration and a fear of failure. At times pieces are missing or distorted because of unhealthy family situations or the influence of normal but still imperfect parents. On the other hand, we as children are also imperfect, and our lack of experience results in our developing a distorted view of reality and relationships.

> Whether we grow up in a fairly healthy family or one with a lot of pain, we all reach adulthood with missing pieces to the puzzle of life and relationships.

Whether we grow up in a fairly healthy family or one with a lot of pain, we all reach adulthood with missing pieces to the puzzle of life and relationships. Great frustration and resentment result when the pieces don't fit together like we think they should or the picture is incomplete because essential pieces just aren't there.

Complicating the matter even further is when we think we've found the missing pieces we're looking for in our spouse. Then to our dismay, we discover our spouse has a lot of the same traits our parents had—traits that helped create the missing pieces we are trying to replace. Go figure! Now our spouse gets the dubious honor of experiencing the frustration and wrath of our past and present.

Another common, yet tragic, mistake is when we go to our spouse to meet needs that only God can fulfill. A spouse can be a positive or negative influence on our sense of self-worth. Yet our basic, most essential need to feel valuable and loved must initially flow out of a personal relationship with Jesus.

CYCLE OF ALIENATION

The process described above often sets up a cyclical response between spouses, which I label the cycle of alienation. This cyclical response creates a downward spiral that begins to unravel the marriage. When this occurs, our spouse responds to our disapproval in one of several ways: fighting back, shutting down, or doing what he or she learned to do during childhood to get approval.

> If the cycle continues and the chasm grows over an extended period of time, basic needs will go unmet, and both spouses will begin to feel hopelessly misunderstood, unloved, and unfairly judged.

But, usually, *what he or she does is not what we need.* Since we don't know how to express what we need, our spouse experiences more disapproval, resulting in feelings of bewilderment. Now our beloved spouse begins to develop a feeling of great injustice, resulting in expressions of frustration, anger, or apathy.

This is a devastating cycle that leaves two committed spouses feeling isolated and alone. Unless missing pieces are identified and the cycle of alienation is reversed, a great chasm will develop in the marriage. If the cycle continues and the chasm grows over an extended period of time, basic needs will go unmet, and both spouses will begin to feel hopelessly misunderstood, unloved, and unfairly judged. When this occurs, either spouse will become a prime target for being susceptible to an affair.

The relationship between Sam and Angela is being eroded by the cycle of alienation. Sam's missing pieces are security, support, and acceptance from those who should have loved him the most—his mom and dad. Angela's missing pieces are acceptance, attention, tenderness, and value that she needed to receive from her father.

By now, both Sam and Angela have learned unhealthy ways to compensate for these missing pieces. Sam learned to work harder to get his deepest longings satisfied. Angela learned to command her dad's, and now her husband's, attention through conflict, although it is not the kind of attention she really longs for.

Now, when Sam feels insecure and criticized, he works harder so Angela will be proud of him. But Angela's deepest need is to know that she is important enough for Sam to set aside work to be with her and the children. When he works harder, it takes him away from the family—the opposite of what Angela needs. The result is that instead of being proud and grateful, Angela becomes critical and caustic like she was with her dad. Sam is confused because what Angela needs feels irresponsible to him, and Angela can't explain it without coming across as angry and unreasonable.

We can all relate to Sam and Angela to some degree. Some of us may feel a lot better about our situation after reading about these two, while others of us are right there with them or worse. An important consideration is the length of time you have been in a cycle of alienation. How many years and how many times have the two of you repeatedly and deeply wounded each other? If you relate to being in this cycle, please seek professional support. This book will alert you to

> An important consideration is the length of time you have been in a cycle of alienation. How many years and how many times have the two of you repeatedly and deeply wounded each other?

some issues and introduce you to some skills, but this book alone will not be enough. While *Safe and Sound* does share insights that will strengthen our marriages, that is not the main goal. The primary purpose is to help us recognize the process of temptation and encourage ministers and their spouses to seek support.

A seasoned professional can assist you in the process of identifying those missing puzzle pieces from your past and the secret codes that keep you from communicating. They can teach you and your spouse new skills that will help each of you complete your individual puzzles and learn to understand the differences in how your hearts interpret love.

DAVID: A CASE STUDY
If it can happen to the best, it can happen to the rest.

The best biblical example of temptation's power over a godly man is King David. Like many of us, David may have come from a decent family, but I'm sure it was far from perfect. Growing up as the youngest of eight boys, it seems David was often overlooked, in some ways left behind, criticized by his older brothers, and later rejected by King Saul. Could it be that during these developmental years, while forming the emotional puzzle pieces of childhood, something was missing? Perhaps he had a need, on an intimate level, to have his sense of value reaffirmed in a way that being king did not satisfy.

"And Samuel said to Jesse, 'Are all the young men here?'" Then he said, 'There remains yet the youngest, and there he is, keeping the sheep'" (1 Sam. 16:11). Can you believe it? The greatest king in the history of Israel was an afterthought in his own household. Later the Scripture tells us his brothers went off to war and he was left behind because of his youth.

In 1 Samuel 17:28, we are privy to a tongue-lashing David received from his oldest brother Eliab. Eliab noticed David among the ranks of Israel and overheard his conversation about Goliath. Eliab assumed David had deserted his responsibilities at home to see the battle: "With whom have you left those few sheep in the wilderness?" (belittling David and his responsibilities in the family). "I know your pride and the insolence of your heart, for you have come down to see the battle." David obviously didn't grow up in the most encouraging family.

In 1 Samuel 18:7, we read that after killing Goliath and subsequent victories over the Philistines, David had risen from the status of shepherd boy to war hero, so the women said as they danced, "Saul has slain his thousands, and David his ten thousands." David was known for his humility before God, but his meteoric ride on the wings of popularity must have had its impact. Perhaps the attention of all the women singing his praises and swooning as he rode by created an appetite for female attention.

Could the need to be noticed and appreciated that went unmet during childhood have played a part in David's moral failure with Bathsheba? Perhaps the taste of popularity on the lips of women dancing in the street also played a part.

Pillar Page

Prayer: "Lord, open my eyes and speak to me, please, just as you did with Jacob. Amen."

❑ As you read this chapter, did any missing pieces to your relationship puzzle come to mind?

❑ Are there some critically important expectations you have of your spouse that have not been clearly verbalized in a respectful manner? *Proverbs 13:12 says, "Hope deferred makes the heart sick."*

❑ Based on your answers to these questions, are you responding to your spouse in ways that create emotional distance?

❑ Would your spouse be open to considering these questions relative to his or her part in the relationship?

❑ Is it possible for the two of you to have a pleasant conversation about your insights and make practical goals to improve your relationship this next week? (Start with the smallest challenges first.)

Phases of the Temptation Process

Phase 1: The Human Condition (Chapter 4)
A mixture of strength and weakness that makes everyone susceptible to enticement. (v. 14 ". . . his own desires . . .")

Phase 2: Enticement (Chapter 5) Opportunity to satisfy a God-given need in an ungodly way. (v. 14 ". . . and enticed . . .")

Phase 3: Conception (Chapter 6) To become pregnant with . . . the birth process of sin begins. One makes a choice to indulge the opportunity before them. Our imagination justifies our behavior. (v. 15 ". . . when desire has conceived, it gives birth to sin.")

Phase 4: Sin Matures (Chapter 7) Compromising behavior is chosen and establishes a pattern that will lead to many destructive choices. (v. 15 "And sin, when it is full-grown . . ." v. 16 "Do not be deceived . . . ")

Phase 5: Sin Manifests (Chapter 8) Subtle compromises become blatant transgressions. The one being tempted becomes more rebellious, blind to consequences, and increasingly careless. (v. 15 ". . . when it is full-grown, brings forth . . .")

James 1:13–16

Let no one say when he is tempted, "I am tempted by God"; for God cannot be tempted by evil, nor does He Himself tempt anyone. But each one is tempted when he is drawn away by his own desires and enticed. Then, when desire has conceived, it gives birth to sin; and sin, when it is full-grown, brings forth death. Do not be deceived, my beloved brethren.

Phase 6: Part 1: Exposure—Discovery (Chapter 9) This phase is characterized by confrontation when that which was done in secret is made known. (v. 15 ". . . brings forth death.")

Phase 6, Part 2: Exposure—Consequences (Chapter 10) All of the consequences become realized. Hearts are broken and dreams are shattered and God's critics are given another reason to blaspheme. (v. 15 ". . . brings forth death. 16Do not be deceived . . .")

CHAPTER 4

The Human Condition (Phase 1 of Temptation)

"Each one is tempted when he is drawn away by his own desires. . ." (James 1:14).

Sam was making his way back across town from a luncheon with the local pastors that met the first Monday of each month.

> **Characteristics of Phase 1:**
> This phase is a mixture of strength and weakness, contentment and neediness, faith and doubt that makes us susceptible to being distracted and led astray by desires that yield to enticement.

He knew he needed to network with these guys, but he despised going. All they ever seemed to talk about was who switched from whose church, what their attendance was on Sunday, and the same church jokes. Sam tried to avoid those conversations because it seemed, as he listened to the others, that his church was the only one in decline. He knew that couldn't be true. Everyone had to be losing members to the towns with newer homes and better jobs.

When Sam turned the corner at Fifth and Elm, he noticed a restaurant that looked like the one he used to manage. Before he realized what he was doing, he had picked up his cell phone. He dialed the old business number like he had a thousand times in what now seemed to be a previous life.

"Italiana's," a familiar voice answered.

"Mike," Sam replied with excitement. "Mike, it's me, Sam, your old manager who gave you his job."

"Sam, is that really you?" said Mike with a tone of recognition. "I can't believe it's you! How's the priesthood and stuff?"

"I'm not a priest," Sam countered. "I'm a pastor."

"Whatever," Mike retorted, not giving it much thought. "Hey, do you play a lot of golf? Some of my buddies told me never to play against a minister because they play golf all week and only work on Sundays."

Sam cringed at that perception of the ministry—Mike hadn't a clue. "Hey, Mike, is anyone still around I know? How's business? You didn't run all my years of success into the ground, did you?"

"The restaurant's doing great, Sam, and I guess the only one still around that you would know is Susan. She's the bartender now. Hey, you want to talk to her? I'm sure she's around here somewhere. In fact, she probably still has the hots for you. You want to talk to her? She still looks as sexy as ever. I can't believe you dumped her for that . . . uh . . . what was her name?"

"Angela, Mike. Her name is Angela," Sam responded with an air of consternation in his voice. "I don't think I want to talk to her, Mike. You can tell her I called. Well, I just wanted to say hello. I passed a restaurant that looked a lot like Italiana's, and before I knew it, I had dialed the number. If you see any customers I know, tell them I said, 'Hello!' See ya, Mike. Have a good day!" Sam hung up the phone feeling more depressed than when he left the pastor's luncheon.

As Sam drove to the church, he could see his former girl-friend, Susan, in his mind, wearing her waitress uniform with the hem that fell halfway up her long, lean thighs. She was a fitness freak, and she had legs that went on forever. She was tall, muscu-lar, and athletic. When she walked by, it was poetry in motion, and her perfume filled the air. Sam could almost smell it. She had beautiful green eyes and flaming red hair, and he could almost taste her flavored lips. . . . "I've got to clear my head," Sam said aloud in a conscious effort to clear the images from his mind. Trying to focus on driving, without success, his thoughts contin-ued, *I know Susan and I were involved, but I haven't thought about a woman in that much detail in a long time.* He shook his head. *Angela and I have got to get our problems worked out!*

Sam called home, and Angela answered, "Hello."

Sam paused for a second and then replied, "Hi, Honey, it's me."

It was odd for Sam to call in the middle of the day, and she noticed something different about the tone of his voice. "Are you OK?" queried Angela.

"I'm fine," he said, "I just talked to Mike back at the old restaurant. I passed a restaurant that looked like Italiana's, so I picked up the phone and called. I was just . . ."

Angela interrupted; the frustration in her voice was obvious. "Are you homesick? You've gotta be kidding? It's a little late for that, don't you think!"

Sam's response was curt and cutting. "I don't know why I try to talk to you. You can tell the kids I'll be home for dinner." Sam hung up and continued down the street to the church office.

Angela's face etched with pain as Sam hung up on her. She sat down at the kitchen table crying. *Why do I do that? Why do I push*

*him away like that? Why couldn't I just listen? Because he makes me so
angry, that's why! How dare he drag us through seminary and out to
a struggling church only to get homesick. He had better not even hint
that any of this might have been a mistake.*

Sam walked into the church office, only to notice that the secretaries were still at lunch. He marched straight to his office and
slammed the door. He sat down and stewed for a few minutes before
opening his E-mail. There on the screen was a message from Karen,
a note of encouragement that read, "You were prayed for today."

This was a surprising but pleasant interruption in the midst
of Sam's frustration, so he quickly typed his response: "Thank
you. This couldn't have come at a better time."

Sam was startled to see an instant message pop up on the
screen, "Why, having a bad day?"

Sam hesitated for a moment, but he needed some encouragement so he replied, explaining how he had called his old workplace and that he and Angela had exchanged words.

Karen's instant message bubble appeared on his screen once
again, reflecting her usual sweet, optimistic attitude in every
word: "I'm sure it was just a misunderstanding. She was probably
having a tough day with the kids. You guys will work it out after
dinner, I'm sure."

Sam typed out his final response, "I sure hope so, Karen. Have
a nice day and I appreciate your support. You're a great friend. I've
got to get some work done, so I'm signing off," and he logged off
the Internet.

Sam had difficulty concentrating the rest of the day. His mind
was awash with emotions and jumbled thoughts. He was sad—
no, angry. He wanted to work, yet he missed the restaurant and

47

old friends. He thought more about his old flame, Susan, and tried to shift his thoughts toward Angela, but he would rather talk to Karen. He felt lonely and frustrated with no one to talk to who would understand.

He wasn't getting anything done, so he hopped in his car and drove to the mall. At least he could be around people and walk around looking at the stores until dinnertime. He wasn't looking forward to going home for dinner. In fact, he was considering any legitimate reason to change his plans and eat out by himself.

Like many of us, Sam has no idea how vulnerable he is at this time in his marriage and his ministry. He also has no idea that Satan's forces have all their preliminary information, have formulated their plan, and are putting it into action.

> We must face the truth that our human condition is a complex design of spiritual potential, emotions, needs, passions, and deep longings or appetites. If our complex design is not addressed in our marriage and our relationship with Jesus Christ, then we are in danger of spiritual attack and moral failure.

Sam and Karen's brief Internet conversation was innocent enough, but it will turn out to be a seed dropped into the fertile soil of Sam and Karen's mutual neediness. Sam knows he is not handling his stress well and that he and Angela are going to have to improve their communication skills, but he has no clue that Karen is a threat.

Sam and Angela's needs go much deeper than a need to communicate better. They have to stop blaming each other and take a long introspective look at themselves. They can't tell each other what they need because they don't know. If they don't understand themselves, how are they going to understand each other?

This is the stage where it would be a counselor's dream for a couple to come in for assistance and say, "We love each other and are committed to each other, but we can't seem to keep from letting each other down. We don't have the marriage we dreamed we would have. We're two intelligent people, but we can't seem to get past this roadblock. Can you help us?"

> "We love each other and are committed to each other, but we can't seem to keep from letting each other down. We don't have the marriage we dreamed we would have. We're two intelligent people, but we can't seem to get past this roadblock. Can you help us?"

What a glorious day that would be! You see, the complexity of relationships and the need to seek help has very little to do with intelligence. It has more to do with having an objective professional listener (a counselor) who is emotionally uninvolved.

His objectivity will allow him to:

- help you identify unmet needs, faulty thinking, and inappropriate responses
- present healthy models for your marriage that may not have been demonstrated anywhere else
- teach you new relational skills to turn the tide in the relationship
- instruct you on how to eliminate the behaviors that are eroding your love for each other

We must face the truth that our human condition is a complex design of spiritual potential, emotions, needs, passions, and deep longings or appetites. If our complex design is not addressed in our marriage and our relationship with Jesus Christ, then we are in danger of spiritual attack and moral failure.

If you choose to remain in your pride and stay determined to handle it yourself, Satan will take notice. He will choose the most opportune time, and he will send enticements to lead you astray.

DAVID: A CASE STUDY
If it can happen to the best, it can happen to the rest.

All of us have needs, insecurities, doubts, fears, and unacceptable desires with which we must contend. Leadership can be a very lonely and stressful place that tends to magnify our weaknesses. It does not matter if you are a king or a pastor; you still have to walk a path that few people understand.

David was no different. He was a man of great character, but not flawless character. David was a handsome, charming, magnetic leader who usually led by example with a unique balance of humility and strength. He was gifted with the sensitivity of a musician and the strength of a warrior. David had a need for intimate relationships, as demonstrated by his friendship with Jonathan (1 Sam. 18:1). It seems David might have been personable and approachable as opposed to the aloof and intimidating persona often attributed to royalty.

However, David was a man of great passion and impulsiveness, as revealed in his dealings with Nabal and Abigail. In this encounter, when David's men were insulted, he rashly vowed to destroy Nabal's family and all he owned. Then as easily as his anger was inflamed, it was assuaged by Abigail's intervention.

When David heard of Nabal's death, he quickly acquired Abigail as his wife. Abigail's beauty and courage obviously had a powerful effect upon David (1 Sam. 25:2–43).

It is clear that David had a notable affinity for women. This, combined with bouts of pride and impulsiveness, would later contribute to a strategic opportunity for his spiritual adversary.

PILLAR PAGE

". . . God is faithful, who will not allow you to be tempted beyond what you are able . . . but . . . will make the way of escape" (1 Cor. 10:13).

Prayer: "Lord, give me the courage to be honest and to obey you by choosing your way of escape. Amen."

- ❏ Based on what you understand about Sam and Angela Bailey's relationship, in what ways do the brief conversations between Sam and Karen pose a threat to Sam's marriage?
- ❏ What are the relational needs Satan will seek to exploit?
- ❏ What are the behaviors Satan might attempt to reinforce?
- ❏ What kind of advice would you share with Angela if she shared the scenario of Sam's phone call with you?
- ❏ What advice would you share with Sam if he asked for your counsel?
- ❏ If you were to change the names and some of the circumstances, could you give yourself some similar counsel to help strengthen your marriage, and avoid temptation?

❏ On the scale below, circle one number to rate the level of satisfaction in your marriage and then on the lower scale note the corresponding level of resistance to temptation.

1　2　3　4　5　6　7　8　9　10
Discontent　　　　　　　　　　Content

10　9　8　7　6　5　4　3　2　1
Highly Vulnerable　　　　Less Vulnerable

Special Note to Minister and Spouse

The scenario being described in the relationship of Sam and Angela is a compilation of common behaviors observed during a process of this nature. The truth is, I could have easily written a scenario where the pastor is preoccupied with the church and the spouse has the affair.

We are all vulnerable and become even more vulnerable when we do not work to make our marriages a rewarding place to be. This relationship must be a priority.

Satan's tactics for destroying marriages are too numerous to mention. Do not be too proud or too private to seek help. If your heart tells you that either of you may be caught in the process of temptation, do not ignore it. Find a way to rock the boat. You may not like getting splashed, but it's better than losing your ship at sea. If your spouse refuses to seek help, then you may need to seek help on your own. One of you getting some guidance is better than none at all.

CHAPTER 5

Enticement
(Phase 2 of Temptation)

"Each one is tempted when he is drawn away . . . and enticed" (James 1:14).

Sam sat at the end of the oval conference table pretending to look at his organizer. He was actually resenting a committee meeting that hadn't even started. While waiting for Roger to call the meeting to order, Sam transitioned between his thoughts and portions of conversations he could hear around the table.

Realizing this was probably going to be another long meeting, Sam tried not to think about the resentment he would feel when he came home late again. He

> **Characteristics of Phase 2:**
> During this phase of temptation, we face the choice of satisfying a God-given need in a godly way or yielding to an unnatural or carnal appetite that has made us its slave.

and Angela no longer fought about it, but now they didn't talk much at all unless it was about the children, the bills, or the tedious details of daily life. There would be no angry words tonight, but neither was Angela going to throw her arms around his neck and welcome him home.

Sam began to glance around the table and take stock of the people who would occupy his life for the next two or three hours. Immediately to Sam's left sat Roger Mumsford, who had agreed to chair this illustrious committee. Roger was a tall man with remnants of superior athletic ability that were displayed when he played on the church basketball team. He had a pleasant demeanor and seemed to enjoy people. Roger was discussing the meeting agenda with Judy Hall, who was sitting immediately to Roger's left. Judy was always very proper and detailed. A single mother with an accounting degree, she was employed by the church part-time as the financial secretary. Judy was prompt, efficient, and able to present the needed financial information well. She hated conflict, however, so she often seemed a little unnerved and intimidated when she was around Mr. Torrence.

Next to Judy sat Steve Lawson. Steve was the youngest and most recently ordained deacon. He was always high-energy and ready to believe God for all the gold in Fort Knox. He had a contagious smile and always managed to point out the positive in every situation. He seemed to be totally oblivious to the fact that he was supposed to cower in the presence of Mr. Torrence, the senior deacon in the church.

These thoughts brought a smirk to Sam's face as he observed Bill Torrence sitting restlessly across from him at the other end of the oval table. It seemed almost as though Mr. Torrence was concerned that Steve's positive view of life might contaminate his seasoned pessimism. Bill was the retired president of the largest and oldest bank in town, but everyone knew that the bank would still answer to him as long as he was alive. He seemed stuck in the 1950s, and he tried to keep the church stuck there right along with him.

Mrs. Wilson sat across from Steve, and they were talking about her flowers. Mrs. Wilson was a sweet elderly lady whose life revolved around her grandchildren and her yard work. She usually seemed clueless during most of the meetings. At times, though, her eyes had a sad look about them as though she was deeply wounded by listening to the endless debate that characterized the meetings. It was when she appeared most wounded that she chose to insert comments filled with profound godly wisdom into the discussion. Although she seemed an enigma in many ways, Sam found himself respecting her as a woman who had spent much time with God.

To her left sat Paul Rayborn, who seemed to shout his way through life—a kindred spirit for Bill Torrence. He and Bill could be quite a pair when they got on a soapbox.

Some key families had been transferred out of town when the aluminum plant closed down. The loss of those families might cause a shortfall in the church's future giving, so this had the potential to be one of those "soapbox" nights.

When Bill and Paul teamed up, Steve's optimism and Roger's calm realism provided a proper balance. Judy usually got quiet, and everything seemed to go right by Mrs. Wilson as though the "soapbox" was not even worthy of notice. Usually Karen's sweet spirit tipped the scale. *Where is Karen?* Sam thought. *She's often a few minutes late, but she's usually here by now. If she doesn't make it, this meeting will be more unbearable than anticipated.*

About the time Sam began to sink another notch into his chair and sulk, he heard Karen's upbeat voice saying, "Good evening" to someone in the hall.

She slipped through the door just as Roger was about to close it. Apologizing as she slid into the only available seat, Karen dropped her stuff by her chair and sighed as she swept her hand across her forehead. "Boy, it feels great to sit still for a moment," she whispered in Sam's direction.

After the prayer, the meeting of numbers and pragmatism was under way. Judy began passing out the monthly financial report. "If this church ever gets any money, the first thing I'm going to do is take the church copier out to an abandoned lot somewhere. Then I'm going to beat it with a sledgehammer," she vented as the papers circulated around the table. "The copier is jammed again, of course, so some of you will have to share."

Sam was the last to receive a copy, so he leaned slightly in Karen's direction and held his report where Karen could see it. The page drooped. She reached up to steady the page, and their forearms touched. Sam could feel the warmth and softness of Karen's skin, and it was soothing to him. Their arms touched for the duration of the five-minute report, but to Sam it felt more like fifteen to twenty minutes.

The instant contact shocked Sam for a second, but then it felt comforting. He felt accepted and encouraged somehow when she didn't adjust her arm immediately to create some space. Then Sam's mind was flooded with thoughts trying to interpret what this meant: *Did it mean anything (she didn't even seem to notice)? She had to notice, but her eyes were focused on Judy the whole time, and she asked good questions. Why didn't she adjust her arm to create some space? She had to feel that! I'm making a big deal out of nothing. Why was this a big deal?* Sam didn't hear much more of the meeting.

Sam continued his attempts to put this moment of incidental touch out of his mind, but he couldn't. It was almost like driving home after a first date, and that felt very uncomfortable because he knew it wasn't right. *I'll just forget it,* he thought. *It was nothing—nothing at all,* he tried to convince himself.

When he got home, he could tell Angela had just gone to bed. The lights were turned out except for the one above the stove that served as a night-light. The scent of the vanilla candle she burned in the kitchen was still wafting in the air even though there was no flame. When he entered the bedroom, he could see the outline of Angela's petite frame under the bedspread. He hung his clothes in the closet, walked into the bathroom, brushed his teeth, and then climbed into bed. Angela was lying on her side with her back to Sam. He leaned over and kissed her on the cheek and said, "Good night."

She had no response, and he lay there wondering if she was really asleep or just pretending. Either way, she seemed very distant. He felt extremely lonely as he drifted off to sleep.

Enticement is a very dangerous

> The persuasion of enticement can either be so subtle that one fails to recognize its influence, or it can be so overwhelming that one is shaken to his very core. When one is caught in its grip, enticement completely captivates the mind and the senses.

and deceptive force, as Sam is finding out. The persuasion of enticement can either be so subtle that one fails to recognize its influence, or it can be so overwhelming that one is shaken to his very core. When one is caught in its grip, enticement completely captivates the mind and the senses. It's like a mind-altering drug that won't leave one's system.

SWEPT AWAY

While living in Florida and regularly visiting the beach, I became acquainted with a phenomenon known as riptide. Riptides or rip currents are usually small channels of water flowing rapidly out to sea occurring near the shore between sandbars or along jetties. They may occur spontaneously with rising tides and winds before or after a storm, or they may be consistently present for months.

A red flag flapping in the breeze off the lifeguard stand means that swimmers are to heed the warnings and stay out of the water. A well-educated swimmer may also recognize the sign of a rip current by observing the water if he is alert. Frequently, though, swimmers either ignore or fail to notice the warnings, and the results are often deadly.

A swimmer might be wading in only waist-deep water when he would be swept off his feet and carried out to sea. It didn't seem to matter if the person was a strong swimmer or in good shape. Eventually the force of the tide would prove too strong, and the swimmer would tire of the fight.

The swimmers who survived the infamous riptides accurately assessed the situation and took appropriate action. The appropriate action was first to admit that the situation was more than they could handle. Second, they conserved their energy by refusing to panic. Third, they signaled for help or knew how to respond appropriately.

If only more pastors and their spouses would follow this strategy when they find themselves caught in the grip of enticement:

- Acknowledge the situation
- Refuse to panic
- Signal for help

ENTICEMENT (PHASE 2 OF TEMPTATION)

Like the swimmer finding himself suddenly swept away in a riptide, the most dangerous moment is when surprise causes one to panic and struggle. Enticement almost always has an element of surprise.

One of the most alarming aspects of enticement is when it awakens appetites and longings one doesn't realize he has. While running an errand to pick up some milk, I entered the grocery store with no sense of hunger. When the sweet pleasant aroma of baking bread drifted my way, suddenly my appetite was awakened, and I had a new understanding of enticement.

> One of the most alarming aspects of enticement is when it awakens appetites and longings one doesn't realize he has.

This magnetic force, like a riptide sweeping away an unsuspecting swimmer, produces the same deadly sensations for its potential victim:

- Power
- Surprise
- Panic
- Isolation
- Persistence

Our human condition consists of longings and appetites. We all experience the power of enticement, but we don't have to drown in it. There are ways to keep from being swept away:

1. Notice the warning signs. Be alert!
2. Don't panic!
3. Admit to yourself the truth of the situation.

4. Respond appropriately.

5. Don't struggle alone. Establish a buddy system or accountability partners to whom you can turn for assistance.

THE WARNING SIGNS

There are recognizable signs that a riptide is present, including darker-colored water, rippling waves, and floating debris. Likewise, there are warning signs that we are being enticed:

- We think about that person more often than usual.
- We're tempted to find incidental reasons to initiate contact.
- Our imagination produces scenarios of what it would be like if this person were our spouse.
- We're disappointed when we expected to see this person and she doesn't show.
- We get excited when this person appears unexpectedly.
- We start paying more attention to our appearance with the prospect of crossing paths with this person during the day.
- When we're in this person's presence, we're tempted to position ourselves closer to her than to others.
- There is usually more incidental touching.
- There is flirtation that is sensed but not easily identified.

Enticement has numerous ways of manifesting itself, and these are only a few of the most common.

Sam and Angela have many negative feelings about their relationship, which increases the power of enticement. When experiencing the attractive thoughts and sensations of enticement while experiencing negative thoughts and sensations with one's spouse, the threat to the marriage is increased exponentially. However, you do not have to be aware of any significant dissatisfaction in your marriage to be enticed by another person.

Don't Panic!

What are the experiences that usually cause panic? Are they not the experiences we least expect to happen to us? For a person truly called of God, I can't think of anything more surprising than to find oneself seriously enticed toward a relationship outside our marriage.

> You do not have to be aware of any significant dissatisfaction in your marriage to be enticed by another person.

We hear about it all the time, but rarely do we believe it can happen to us. Yes, we'll admit that it can, but we don't believe it will. A minister does not answer the call to ministry expecting to be tempted by adultery any more than a young couple gets married expecting to divorce. Yet both of these tragic events happen more often than we realize.

What then shall we do? The swimmers who avoid being swept away by a riptide are those who understand the power of the sea and the potential for anyone, including themselves, to be swept away. Those who ignore the lifeguard's red flags and think they do not apply to them are the ones who get swept away.

> It seems too often that pastors are unwilling to admit to themselves that, like riptides in the sea, enticement is a natural phenomenon of the human condition.

No matter how called, anointed, or prepared we feel we may be, we must never underestimate the weakness of the human condition. This is why Paul warns us in Galatians 6:1, "Considering yourself lest you also be tempted."

ADMIT TO YOURSELF THE TRUTH OF THE SITUATION

"No temptation has overtaken you except such as is common to man" (1 Cor. 10:13).

The swimmers who drown in a riptide are those who fail to admit to themselves the true strength of the current. Therefore, they do not respond properly to the situation. They try to swim directly against the current in a panic response. The wise swimmer recognizes that riptides are a natural phenomenon of the sea and, if responded to appropriately, do not have to be life threatening.

However, it seems too often that pastors are unwilling to admit to themselves that, like riptides in the sea, enticement is a natural phenomenon of the human condition. The male/female chemistry of attraction does not cease to exist simply because we are married, and neither is it limited only to our spouses. The ability to attract male/female attention or to discover sudden chemistry with the opposite sex assuredly continues.

> The male/female chemistry of attraction does not cease to exist simply because we are married, and neither is it limited only to our spouses. The ability to attract male/female attention or to discover sudden chemistry with the opposite sex assuredly continues.

Like the riptides, most of the time this chemistry is manageable and non-threatening. Be aware, though, that under certain conditions, both can be very dangerous. Riptides are strongest at high tide and in times of recent or building storms. Likewise, the chemistry of attraction is likely to be overwhelming during times of stress or conflict. We are especially vulnerable when there is a sense of rejection in the marital relationship. These are the times when our need for approval, comfort, or support can sweep us away into an illicit relationship.

RESPOND APPROPRIATELY

"But God is faithful, who will not allow you to be tempted beyond what you are able, but . . . will also make the way of escape, that you may be able to bear it" (1 Cor. 10:13b).

An educated swimmer knows how to respond when caught in a riptide. He understands that he will either need assistance or that the current should eventually dissipate, allowing him to swim out of its path. In a similar fashion, pastors must understand that when they find themselves experiencing the wayward undertow of enticement, it should dissipate if they do not respond. However, if the current proves too strong and too persistent, they must signal for assistance.

A common tip for swimmers wishing to avoid an unwanted trip out to sea is always to swim under the supervision of a lifeguard. In the same way, it is imperative that every pastor have lifeguards in his life. These lifeguards should be people who know him and his ministry and who have enough authority and understanding to lovingly hold him accountable. These are people with whom one can be completely transparent and vulnerable. They know how to keep a confidence. It is not difficult to notice other members of the congregation or community who exhibit

> These lifeguards should be people who know him and his ministry and who have enough authority and understanding to lovingly hold him accountable.

maturity, wisdom, and compassion. However, they must need to know how to be stern and uncompromising when necessary.

In Galatians 5:13, Paul warns, "Do not use liberty as an opportunity for the flesh." Paul also admonishes us in Galatians 6 to take heed lest we be tempted to fall into a trespass or to think too highly of ourselves, leading to self-deception. Those who attempt a lasting ministry without lifeguards are acting foolishly and are truly deceived. They do not accurately discern the treacherous conditions of their environment, and they are at great risk of being swept away.

David: A Case Study
If it can happen to the best, it can happen to the rest.

"In the spring, at the time when kings go off to war, David sent Joab out with the king's men and the whole Israelite army. They destroyed the Ammonites and besieged Rabbah. But David remained in Jerusalem. One evening David got up from his bed and walked around on the roof of the palace. From the roof, he saw a woman bathing. The woman was very beautiful" (2 Sam. 11:1–2 NIV).

Enticement can strike suddenly with almost no warning, or it can build over time as it simmers just below the surface. I have often wondered which scenario it was with David and Bathsheba.

On the one hand, David seemed to be in a state of mind conducive for temptation while not necessarily looking for trouble. The reason he seemed vulnerable was because David was not with his soldiers in battle like the rest of the kings, as was his normal practice. Also, while David's men had given up the comforts of home, he was taking a nap and attempting to refresh himself by walking on the roof of his house. Was David depressed? Was he bored and unmotivated? Had his success created a situation where he no longer felt challenged?

Whatever the reasoning, David was not where he should have been, nor was he doing what God had anointed him to do. It seems he was not focused on being God's servant as king, but rather on serving himself. When he suddenly caught a view of Bathsheba bathing, Satan seized the moment. The spiritual forces that sought to destroy God's work in David's life began to work through the king's affinity for women, his impulsiveness, and the assumptions of privilege (in which David was indulging by not going to battle and lounging in his house). Suddenly David was under attack, and just as suddenly he was felled by his unguarded heart and an unexpected opportunity.

On the other hand, had David possibly noticed Bathsheba before? Could it have been a regular practice of the king to peer down from his housetop and watch women bathe? Is it possible that this was David's form of Internet pornography? If this was the case, then enticement's blow was not sudden but simmering in nature. Perhaps David knew it was common for Bathsheba to bathe at that time of the evening and knew what he was anticipating when he walked out on the roof. If this was the case, then Satan simply studied David's behavior and set a plan in motion. David had never pursued Bathsheba before. Something had changed.

Whether acting on impulse or under the compulsiveness of simmering passion, for the first time David felt free to inquire about Bathsheba's identity. Could it be that all of David's accountability relationships (his lifeguards) were in battle against Ammon where David should have been?

Pillar Page

"God is faithful, who will not allow you to be tempted beyond what you are able . . . but . . . will also make the way of escape" (1 Cor. 10:13).

Prayer: "Lord, give me the courage to be honest and to obey you by choosing your way of escape. Amen."

Enticement defined: The awakening of inappropriate desire that is persistent and enduring in nature, thus requiring exceptional amounts of mental, emotional, and spiritual resources to resist.

- ❏ Have you ever experienced enticement of this magnitude?
- ❏ Do you have lifeguards in place to whom you can turn in all honesty for support? If the answer is yes, who are they? (They need to be people of integrity whom you can trust to keep a confidence and who have enough authority to challenge your behavior. Hint: These are people who are sought out by members of your church or community for advice or counsel. They may or may not be members of your congregation.)
- ❏ If the answer is no, who might qualify to be your lifeguards?
- ❏ Although it would be uncomfortable, is your marital relationship such that you could share your struggle with your spouse?
- ❏ If the struggle with enticement is affecting your marriage, would you consider seeking the assistance of a professional counselor on how to approach this issue?

WORD TO THE WISE

Secrets equal sickness. Secrets leave us free to indulge further, and they sabotage intimacy with our spouse.

Now is the optimal time to seek help and support. At this phase of the temptation process, one is only confessing weakness. Every phase after this involves increasing levels of moral failure and increasingly painful consequences.

CHAPTER 6

Conception
(Phase 3 of Temptation)

"When desire has conceived, it gives birth to sin" (James 1:15).

"The touch" occurred in the business meeting on Tuesday evening, and Sam had managed not to have any direct contact with Karen on Wednesday or Thursday.

> **Characteristics of Phase 3:**
> During this phase the birth process of sin begins. A person makes a choice to indulge the opportunity before him, first in thought and then in action. Personal imagination justifies the rebellious heart and rationalizes behavior as harmless and inconsequential.

Sam struggled for two days trying to get that moment of incidental touch with Karen out of his head, but it was driving him crazy. He could focus on work for short periods of time, but he had to use all of his extra mental energy to keep pushing the incident to the back of his mind. Yet the sense of warmth, acceptance, comfort, and encouragement that he felt from one incidental touch refused to take its proper seat in the unconscious. He thought about calling Karen several times for one thing or another, but he knew he really shouldn't.

Friday morning, after his coffee break, Sam logged on to the Internet to look at some recent changes to the church's Web site. He was greeted with an E-mail from Karen. At first he was hesitant to read it, but eventually he opened the simple message that read like the last one, "You were prayed for today."

At this point he began to wrestle with himself. *Do I reply or delete, reply or delete, reply or delete* . . . until finally the mouse clicked "Reply."

Sam's fingers typed out a message that was appropriate enough, but his emotions were much stronger and much more confused. "Thank you for the prayer, and I hope you have a great weekend. I look forward to seeing you in church on Sunday. Sam." He pushed "Send" and then returned to examining the changes on the church's Web site. Sam thought to himself, *This site isn't much, but at least our little church has a presence in this virtual world. I'll bet we're the only church in town that even has a Web site.* Feeling a sense of pride, he began using the search engine to see if any of the other churches in town had a presence on the Web.

Sam was startled (and delighted) when an instant message from Karen popped on the screen. "I noticed you were on-line, so I thought I would say hello. I'm almost finished with my proposal for the budget and finance committee regarding the remodeling of the youth house. Do you mind if I attach it to an E-mail so you can look over it? I would really like to know what you think. Karen."

"I would be glad to look at it," Sam replied. "We want to be prepared because the teens really need a place they feel belongs to them, but you know Mr. Torrence will be against it."

A cute reply came back, "You got that right. That man would be against his own funeral if he still had a vote." They joked back and forth for a minute, and then Sam began to be aware of the time, so they signed off.

The weekend passed by in normal fashion. Sam and Angela kept their pace of running errands and getting the kids where they needed to go. Jon had a karate tournament that took up most of the day, and Tommy had an evening baseball game that would make it a late night. By the time they got the kids bathed and in bed, it would be after ten o'clock. Then Sam would look over his messages for Sunday, and Angela would get everyone's clothes ready for the following morning. Finally they would collapse in bed exhausted and be unconscious before their heads hit their pillows.

Sunday was a blur, of course. It always was. Neither Sam nor Angela really minded the pace because it gave them some semblance of family time, and there was never any time for conflict. Silence and family business had become the language of their relationship.

Monday morning when Sam got to the office, he turned on his computer to find Karen's E-mail with the remodeling proposal attached. Sam took about thirty minutes to look over it and then began to formulate his response. He hesitated for a moment before he began the E-mail. *I think I'll call her. It will take me forever to type this, and calling would be much easier.*

The truth is, he thought it would be nice to hear her voice. There was always a lift in her voice that picked up his spirits. Sam was always a little depressed on Mondays anyway. Eventually Sam would find a good reason to call Karen almost every Monday. She was so involved in the church that there was always some issue to discuss.

This would be the beginning of a constant flow of communication between Sam and Karen: E-mails, phone calls, and extended conversations after committee meetings. Following the remodeling project for the youth house was the big seventy-fifth anniversary for the church. Karen had agreed to head up the planning committee, which would require a lot of time to organize and coordinate. Karen and Sam would be in constant contact throughout the months it would take to plan the event.

The church wanted this anniversary celebration to be the biggest and best ever. They doubted that any of the charter members would still be around for another quarter of a century. They also wanted to extend an invitation to every pastor who had served the church since its illustrious beginnings. This was going to require a lot of energy and time. Even Mr. Torrence, a charter member, expressed his approval. Sam really had no choice but to give this event all the attention he could afford—and he did.

BREAK THE SILENCE—SEEK SUPPORT!

We know we are being enticed with the awakening of desire—desire we know is inappropriate. Often we are vulnerable to such temptation because basic needs are going unmet in our marital relationships. However, one may be enticed simply because of the common weakness of the human condition even when the marriage is quite sound. Whatever may be the reason for our enticement, if we allow it to go unchecked, the process will progress to the next phase—the conception of sin. Undisciplined thoughts, feelings, and imagination will produce inappropriate actions.

We must not fail to realize that the awakening of desire is our warning that we are being enticed. This is the optimal time to reach out to our lifeguards (accountability partners) for assistance. The greater the intensity and the greater the potential for failure, based on personal history, the more support a person will need.

Seeking support from our trusted lifeguards accomplishes two essential purposes in our struggle to prevent temptation from gaining more territory in our lives:

- First, it garners prayer support to empower us against spiritual attack.
- Second, it destroys the sense of isolation and the power of secrecy.

> We must not fail to realize that the awakening of desire is our warning that we are being enticed. This is the optimal time to reach out to our lifeguards (accountability partners) for assistance.

We must not forget or underestimate the spiritual forces that are at work when Satan is trying to move us from simply being tempted to sinful behavior. It is at this crucial moment that we need people (lifeguards) praying for us as Paul did for the believers in the young church at Ephesus:

For this reason I bow my knees to the Father . . . that He would grant you, according to the riches of His glory, to be strengthened with might through His Spirit in the inner man, . . . that you, being rooted and grounded in love, may be able to comprehend with all the saints what is the width and length and depth and height—to know the love of Christ which passes knowledge, that you may be

filled with all the fullness of God . . . according to
the power that works in us, to Him be glory . . .
Amen (Eph. 3:14–21).

Sin has not conceived until you commit your heart to sinful
action. Proverbs 29:18 states, "Where there is no revelation, the
people cast off restraint." At this critical

> **Sin has not conceived until you commit your heart to sinful action.**

juncture in the temptation process, Satan
is attempting to cloud our vision and
blind us with desire, so we will lose sight
of what God is attempting to do in us and through us.

It is crucial that we have lifeguards praying for God's Spirit
to fill us with the fullness of God so that we may comprehend the
love of Christ for us. Our awareness of the Father's love for us in
Jesus Christ is our greatest deterrent to temptation. This is why
Paul wrote to the Corinthian church, "The love of Christ com-
pels us, . . . that those who live should

> **The key to resisting temptation is not regulation but relationship.**

live no longer for themselves, but for
Him who died for them and rose again"
(2 Cor. 5:14–15). Righteousness that
arises out of love has always produced more purity in God's servants than rules. The key to resisting temptation is not regulation
but relationship.

SATAN'S SECRET WEAPONS

Satan is always trying to erode our relationship with the heavenly Father. He uses every weapon at his disposal, and the intensity is often greatest at the most strategic moments in our spiritual
journey. If we do not falter, it is often at that moment that we

reach the precipice of a spiritual breakthrough. Didn't Jesus cry out, "My God, My God, why hast thou forsaken me?" (KJV) just before he yielded up his spirit to make the purchase of our salvation complete? (Matt. 27:46–51).

Two of Satan's most effective weapons are shame and self-pity. Both of these weapons flourish in an environment of secrecy and isolation. Therefore, our response to temptation must be to tell trusted individuals what we are experiencing in order to change our environment to one of openness and support. When we break the isolation, we destroy the power of secrecy and Satan's ability to blackmail the saints of God through false accusations and lies. The apostle John records, "For the accuser of our brethren has been thrown down, who accuses them before our God day and night. And they overcame him because of the blood of the Lamb and because of the word of their testimony, and they did not love their life even to death" (Rev. 12:10b–11 NASB).

> Both of these weapons flourish in an environment of secrecy and isolation. Therefore, our response to temptation must be to tell trusted individuals what we are experiencing in order to change our environment to one of openness and support.

Satan attempts to accuse us and use the power of secret sin to destroy us. His desire is to fill us with self-pity, creating a feeling of overwhelming loneliness and absence of genuine love.

One of the most common uses of self-pity is to fill us with shame. Satan leads us to feel so disgusted with ourselves that we stop pursuing righteousness and purity. Due to past sins, Satan convinces us that we are hopelessly damaged goods, and therefore, we might as well indulge. The lie we believe is this: "At least we'll get the immediate pleasure, and we're already hopelessly damaged—so why not?"

However, in this discussion, self-pity is more than thoughts of self-loathing and absence of personal value. With these elements of self-pity, there is also a tendency toward "injustice thinking." Injustice thinking concludes that we are getting shortchanged in our marriage and getting a raw deal in the life we are living. We begin to believe that we are being undervalued by everyone except the one who has proven himself or herself worthy of our attention and desire.

When this way of thinking is accepted as truth, then we start telling ourselves what we deserve and what we shouldn't have to put up with or do without. Once we begin acting on these lies, our relationship with God and our spouse begins to unravel. It is only a matter of time until our ministry begins to suffer as well.

> Once we begin acting on these lies, our relationship with God and our spouse begins to unravel.

At this point, we begin to lose sight of our moral markers, making everything relative. There is no more black and white or right and wrong. All is gray, and everything is relative. Since no one knows the severity of our situation, they cannot understand and therefore they have no counsel to offer us. At this point, the schemes of the devil have manipulated us into the spiritual darkness where the sinful bent of our flesh can flourish. Then the flesh—our sinful habits and the desires we have to meet our needs apart from the power of God—grows stronger while the influence of our reborn spirit and the Holy Spirit grows weaker.

Oswald Chambers in *My Utmost for His Highest* states, "Self-pity is of the devil; if I go off on that line I cannot be used by God for His purpose in the world."

> The optimal time to take advantage of such support is immediately upon realizing that you are being enticed— *before* desire conceives sin.

When Satan is dealing with gifted leaders, he will use a tactic on the opposite end of the spectrum from self-pity. He will use self-indulgent pride. A man's sense of value can become overinflated, causing him to feel invulnerable to the consequences that sin imposes on others. One begins to feel as if the rules that apply to others somehow do not apply to him. Now, of course, a minister would never admit he thinks this way, but the truth is displayed in his actions.

Seeking Support Is Still the Best Solution

The Tempter knows that when intense desire and overwhelming self-pity cause us to lose sight of what God is doing, we become unrestrained. We are capable of doing anything. The same is also true when we feel we are above the rules. However, if we have trusted lifeguards with whom we can share our secrets, then Satan can't isolate us. Also, when our lifeguards love us in spite of our weaknesses, pray for us, and speak God's truth into our lives, then Satan cannot fill us with lies of self-pity and condemnation. These guardians can also be very effective at keeping us in our rightful place when others seek to exalt us.

You must realize that Satan will do everything he can to convince you not to seek out lifeguards. He will use self-indulgent pride to convince you they are not necessary.

Is this not the principle of which Solomon spoke in his God-given wisdom in Ecclesiastes 4:9–12? "Two are better than one. . . . If one falls down, his friend can help him up. But pity the man who falls and has no one to help him up. . . . Though one may be overpowered, two can defend themselves. A cord of three strands is not quickly broken" (NIV). Everyone needs spiritual support upon whom they can call with complete honesty. The optimal time to take advantage of such support is immediately upon realizing you are being enticed—*before* desire conceives sin.

SIGNS OF CONCEPTION

How does a person know when he is at this crucial stage in the temptation process? There will be several signs:

- Increased intensity of desire
- Fixed obsession
- Mental gymnastics to justify one's chosen course of action

The Greek word for "desire" is *epithumia*, meaning a longing for what is forbidden. This is often a strong lustful desire that is sexual in nature. The imagery is that of being consumed or burning up with passion or craving (Rom. 1:27). Perhaps "lust" would be a more accurate translation than "desire."

Notice how Genesis describes Eve's craving for the forbidden fruit when sin was conceived: "So when the woman saw that the tree was good for food, that it was pleasant to the eyes, and . . . desirable . . . she took" (Gen. 3:6). In similar fashion, 1 John 2:16 teaches, "For all that is in the world—the lust of the flesh, the lust of the eyes, and the pride of life—is not of the Father but is of the world." Did you notice the fixation of Eve on the forbidden fruit and the complete focus of the senses described in 1 John? This obsession takes more and more of our mental energy as we pass from enticement to conception.

Immediately following obsession, justification begins to take place. One will think of himself as doing something noble. We might picture ourselves as the rescuer delivering the person of our obsession from a relationship that is unworthy of her, or providing her with the love she has always deserved.

But the Book of Proverbs is quite clear about this process and its consequences:

- "His own iniquities entrap the wicked man, and he is caught in the cords of his sin. He shall die for lack of instruction, and in the greatness of his folly he shall go astray" (Prov. 5:22–23).
- "The righteousness of the upright will deliver them, but the unfaithful will be taken by their lust" (Prov. 11:6).
- "There is a way that seems right to a man, but its end is the way of death" (Prov. 14:12).

> When this phase of temptation is complete, then our lust will have become manifest in actions that may appear appropriate at first; but as time passes, they will become obviously inappropriate to everyone but us.

When this phase of temptation is complete, then our lust will have become manifest in actions that may appear appropriate at first; but as time passes, they will become obviously inappropriate to everyone but us. By this point in the process, it will be likely that we have completely committed ourselves to the deception.

The time will come, however, when the process of temptation is complete, and humiliation and pain will clear our thinking. Deception will have run its course, the fog will lift, and we will be able to see clearly the moments of decision that led us astray. These are known as decision points.

Sam's decision points were the choices to click "reply" rather than "delete" on his E-mail and when he chose to call Karen in order to hear her voice over the phone.

These actions in and of themselves would have been harmless. But combine these actions with emotional neediness and the wrong motives—and these few sparks can set a forest ablaze.

CONSEQUENCES

Now that some degree of indulgence has taken place, the marriage has been compromised. Aggressive measures need to be taken to cut off or completely minimize contact with this person. This person is now a threat that has begun to encroach on the unity of the marriage.

We must realize that this is not just an individual problem. This is a marital problem and is rapidly becoming a church problem. Deception and a series of choices have resulted in the violation of a spouse's trust.

> **We must realize that this is not just an individual problem. This is a marital problem and is rapidly becoming a church problem.**

Counselors differ in their judgments on when and how much disclosure is appropriate. However, secrets create barriers to true intimacy, and a lack of intimacy is a great contributor to the relationship's vulnerability.

If we choose to be honest, we would be wise not to expect a big hug and a kiss for doing the right thing. Our spouse will probably be hurt and angry before she is appreciative. While telling the truth may be doing the right thing, it should have been done sooner.

Now trust will have to be rebuilt, and this is not an easy task. It will take time and a lot of effort on the part of both spouses. Fortunately, this is still much better than allowing the temptation process to progress further.

DAVID: A CASE STUDY

If it can happen to the best, it can happen to the rest.

"And David sent someone to find out about her. The man said, 'Isn't this Bathsheba, the daughter of Eliam and the wife of Uriah the Hittite?'" (2 Sam. 11:3 NIV).

When David responded to the magnetic draw of enticement, he moved impulsively into the next phase of temptation. Conception occurred when David put action to his thoughts and desires.

The actions taken at this point in the process are obvious and may even seem innocent at first; but the true motivation that drives each choice makes them deadly.

What was David thinking when he decided to inquire about this young woman's identity? Had he already decided that he must have her, or had he lied to himself by thinking, *What harm does it do to know the name of this woman? Is it a crime for me to satisfy my curiosity?* When sin has been conceived, a person becomes less receptive to wise counsel. Only a few people would have been able to get David's attention at this stage.

It seems that one of David's servants may have asked a question in such a way as to imply the inappropriate nature of David's inquiry, "Is this not Bathsheba, the daughter of Eliam, the *wife* of Uriah the Hittite?" (NIV, emphasis added). However, this person did not have the authority to challenge the king about his behavior.

David needed a lifeguard; but none were to be found. Now, because of his "harmless" inquiry, he had the piece of information that would lead him further down temptation's path. Not only was Bathsheba beautiful, but she would be alone for an extended period of time.

Pillar Page

"God is faithful, who will not allow you to be tempted beyond what you are able . . . but . . . will also make the way of escape" (1 Cor. 10:13).

Prayer: "Lord, give me the courage to be honest and to obey you by choosing your way of escape. Amen."

❑ What was the decision point in Sam's struggle with enticement that caused sin to be conceived? What were the choices that led to that decisive moment?

❑ What were the symptoms or behaviors that would lead you to conclude that sin had clearly taken hold in Sam Bailey's life?

❑ Can you or someone you know relate to Sam's struggle and poor choices?

❑ Are there secrets in your life that Satan uses to blackmail you into self-pity?

❏ Has God blessed you with some incredible talents? Might Satan use pride to lead you astray?

❏ What are the lies spoken into your thoughts to convince you to struggle alone?

• No one will understand.

• If anyone knows that about you, he or she will be disgusted by you.

• If you tell anyone this is a problem, he or she will never respect you again.

• If you tell anyone about this, you'll be fired for sure.

• No one will love you if they know the truth about you.

• You can handle it; why share those thoughts with people who look up to you?

• Others:_____

_____

_____

_____

_____

❏ Instead of struggling alone, what are some appropriate actions to take?

❏ How would this be more difficult, now that one is further along in the temptation process?

CHAPTER 7

Sin Matures (Phase 4 of Temptation)

"Sin, when it is full-grown . . . Do not be deceived" (James 1:15–16).

During the next few months Sam was only home enough to keep Angela satisfied, which didn't take much anymore. He made sure he was at all of the boys' activities and watched TV or read a book to Sara before he left for the office in the mornings. Sam and Angela were intimate on a few occasions—futile attempts to recapture something. Both sensed the emptiness, but neither of them said anything. The physical touch was nice enough, but there was no passion, and the light in their eyes was gone.

> **Characteristics of Phase 4:**
> A person chooses compromising behavior, and this establishes a pattern that will lead to many destructive choices. At this stage, it is almost impossible to get the individuals involved to recognize or admit to wrongdoing.

Sam had begun to feel self-conscious about all the E-mail conversations with Karen, so he collected the E-mail addresses of other committee members and found reasons to E-mail them as well. He was also concerned about catching flack from Angela if he used the cell phone too much. So he bought some calling cards and a second cell phone (for regional use only), which he charged to his expense account with the church. Like the E-mail usage, Sam found reasons to call other church leaders so he wouldn't draw attention to how much time he and Karen spent on the phone.

Of course, none of this was very difficult with all the excitement and planning for the seventy-fifth anniversary of the church. Karen was in charge of everything, so it was obvious that she and the pastor would need to keep each other abreast of the details and how things were progressing. If Angela asked about the second phone, he could say it was necessary to save money for the church with all the extra calling required for the big event.

One afternoon, after the senior adult Bible study and luncheon, Sam was making small talk with Mrs. Wilson about her flowers, the grandchildren, and the upcoming anniversary celebration. Mrs. Wilson was about to walk away when she turned and placed her fragile hand on Sam's arm. Looking up at him with eyes of deep compassion and a tone of caution, she said, "Sam, you work long hours at this church. I noticed that you and Karen enjoy each other's company. Remember that Peter was not the only disciple that Satan would like to sift as wheat."

Stunned, Sam managed a "yes ma'am." He stood there as she patted his arm then slowly left the room. At first Sam wondered if she knew something, but he eventually convinced himself she was just a sweet elderly lady.

It wasn't uncommon, and actually it had become fairly routine, for Karen to wait until all her planning committee members had gone home and then make her way to Sam's office, deceiving herself as she went. *There is nothing physical going on; we just have things to talk about,* she continued deceiving herself. *Sam is witty and fun. He makes me laugh and he listens to me. I'll only stay for a few minutes and then I'll go home,* she promised herself as she entered the church office, hoping Sam was still there.

They had never discussed these meetings. They just somehow became routine, and of course, Sam could always find work to do. They would talk and share a cup of coffee as the time slipped away.

SELF-DECEPTION

Sin is often so subtle and the deception so great that we are blind to the changes in our behavior that accommodate our sin. Each compromising step in the wrong direction is matched by an equally deceptive excuse. So complete is the deception that those involved in an affair are shocked when the relationship moves beyond what they expected.

When Sam collected the E-mail addresses of other church leadership, his real motive was to cover up his time on the Internet with Karen. This, however, is not what he told himself. He convinced himself that others would not understand how much coordination this event required and he didn't have time for such petty criticism.

Likewise, he justified the calling cards and the extra phone as an issue of how unreasonable Angela could be. He was not hiding his relationship with Karen; he was avoiding a fight with his unreasonable wife. After all, he and Karen were just good friends who worked well together, and they knew how to get things done, or so he would tell himself. It's not as if anything sexual were going on.

Most of us rarely stop to consider the dynamics of relation-ships and how people develop intimacy, so these dynamics go unnoticed. But they are very influential and very real. For example, on a nice spring day, a light breeze may go unnoticed beyond a momentary thought, but its constant flow moves the clouds along throughout the day and eventually will bring in a storm system.

When people are lonely, stressed, insecure, bored, or just in need of some attention, they enjoy the company of someone whose presence provides what they need. They don't know why; they just know they feel better about themselves when this person is around. The attention this person provides makes them feel like they can accomplish more or that everything will be all right. If this person is of the opposite sex, they may simply make us feel more attractive or clever.

> Boundaries are the understood limitations of a relationship; they define the appropriate interactions that keep the limitations in place.

All of this seems innocent enough until the chemistry we feel with this per-son is something we begin to depend on.

In this case, we will begin to find subtle reasons to be in his or her presence that will become increasingly obvious with time. This increasingly consistent interaction will set in motion certain relational dynamics that neither is aware of.

BOUNDARIES

The building blocks of intimacy are often already in place whether or not the people involved are aware of them. Intimacy will cause the relationship to change constantly and to progress to a deeper level. This is why every relationship with the opposite sex needs to have proper boundaries.

Boundaries are the understood limitations of a relationship; they define the appropriate interactions that keep the limitations in place. Intimacy is not limited to sexual relationships. Intimacy occurs whenever two people freely share themselves with each other through the exchange of ideas, resources, and experience.

This is why so many bosses run off with their secretaries. The boss and his secretary become a team sharing ideas, goals, and experience. If limitations are not clearly defined within the relationship, there is always a chance the level of intimacy can become inappropriate. The greatest defense against this potential disaster on the part of the boss is a deep, healthy, and intimate relationship with his wife, which will dictate that he create an appropriate professional working relationship with his secretary.

BUILDING THE CONNECTION

The four building blocks of intimacy that make possible the dynamics necessary for a deepening relationship are the intellectual, the emotional, the physical, and the spiritual:

The *intellectual* is the freedom to share one's thoughts freely without fear of ridicule or rejection and a high probability of acceptance.

The *emotional* is the desire and the freedom to reveal how we feel without fear that our transparency will be used against us and in all likelihood will be rewarded with greater understanding.

The *physical* often involves the sexual component but not necessarily. If it does, the sexual is part of the greater "whole" of feeling protected and provided for appropriately.

The *spiritual* is the freedom to share personal revelations of truth from God and about God, as well as the celebration of our relationship with him.

Affairs that involve genuine relationship and intimacy usually begin with intellectual or emotional sharing that continues over an extended period of time. The length of time it takes for the affair to show itself will depend on the neediness of the couple and the intensity of the situation. Some relationships seem to occur almost spontaneously, while others take years to develop.

> The length of time it takes for the affair to show itself will depend on the neediness of the couple and the intensity of the situation. Some relationships seem to occur almost spontaneously, while others take years to develop.

WARNING: HIGH RISK

One would think that with the values of the faith community and the commitment of the people to God's authority, affairs would be less likely in the ministry. Yet I contend that the ministry in many ways has a greater probability of infidelity than most business situations.

Following are a few of the reasons why:

- A lack of a clear definition exists between personal life and ministerial life.
- The nature of the ministry causes a minister to be involved in other people's lives at a variety of levels.
- There is usually maximum freedom and minimal (if any) accountability for use of time or whereabouts.
- Relationships tend to be more causal rather than professional.

• The process of intimacy often begins with the spiritual element (the most intimate of all four basic elements) or the emotional element, both of which are incredibly powerful and binding.

This is what has occurred with Sam and Karen. She enjoys Sam's company because she values the spiritual leadership that does not exist in her marriage. Sam appreciates Karen because she values his opinion and she listens to his ideas. They do not realize the power of these two building blocks of intimacy, especially when they are lacking in their relationship with their spouses.

The dynamics of intimacy, mutual neediness, extended time together, and no accountability will prove to be a toxic combination for Sam and Karen. This type of environment is highly conducive for the development of unexpected affairs.

THREE LAWS OF RELATIONSHIPS

An affair is unexpected because not only are Sam and Karen, like most of us, unaware of the dynamics of intimacy, but they are also unaware of three basic laws of relationship.

> Each time Sam chooses to E-mail, call, or visit with Karen for support instead of his wife, he invests in his relationship with Karen and diminishes the value of his relationship with Angela.

The first law is the *law of investment.* Jesus stated in his Sermon on the Mount, "For where your treasure is, there your heart will be also" (Matt. 6:21).

In this discourse, Jesus was challenging his disciples to invest their lives in God's heavenly kingdom rather than an earthly kingdom. The truth he shares is, of course, just as simple as it is profound: A person's heart and his affections will follow his investment.

This truth not only applies to wealth but also to emotional investment, intellectual investment, spiritual investment, and physical investment. Do you get the picture? Each time Sam chooses to E-mail, call, or visit with Karen for support instead of his wife, he invests in his relationship with Karen and diminishes the value of his relationship with Angela.

This leads to the second law of relationship—the *law of evolution*. Relationships, like people, are meant to evolve, develop, and mature. Relationships do not remain stagnant. They change, whether they become stronger or weaker, depending on one's pattern of investment.

While Sam and Karen say there is nothing inappropriate about their relationship, this won't be their situation for long. The deadly combination of interactions mentioned earlier will rapidly change the nature of their relationship.

> Not only does the intensity of the conflict between two competing relationships increase, but eventually the heart will have to choose.

This is why Jesus said, when discussing the heart's inability to serve two masters, "Either he will hate the one and love the other, or he will hold to one and despise the other" (Matt. 6:24 NASB).

The more Sam invests in his relationship with Karen, the more he will resent his relationship with Angela. At the present time, Angela is an inconvenience to be worked around, but eventually Sam may see his relationship with Angela as the only thing standing in the way of his true happiness with Karen.

If Sam and Karen's relationship is allowed to evolve to this level, then Angela will begin to realize that their marriage is being handicapped by more than work, resentment, and poor communication. If she attempts to appeal to Sam about her concerns, he will become increasingly more difficult to talk with. Sam may become defensive and rude, maybe even aggressive. He may even blow her off altogether, attempting to make her feel silly or paranoid. That is, until she finds some indisputable proof.

By the end of the maturing phase of temptation, law three of relationships will be in place: the *law of limited loyalty*. Not only does the intensity of the conflict between two competing relationships increase, but eventually the heart will have to choose. Jesus made it quite clear that "no one can serve two masters" (Matt. 6:24). Our hearts cannot equally serve two competing loyalties. Eventually we will honor one and violate the other.

> I have seen men and women try to defy these laws of relationships time and time again to their own destruction. Solomon wrote in Proverbs 18:1, "A man who isolates himself seeks his own desire; he rages against all wise judgment."

Jesus was discussing the competing loyalty between serving God and serving money, but the law holds true for every relationship. The law of limited loyalty is that our hearts are designed for only one loyalty. This is why Jesus also said, "Because of the hardness of your heart [Moses] wrote you this precept [certificate of divorce]. But from the beginning of the creation, God 'made them male and female' . . . 'and the two shall become one flesh.' . . . no longer two, but one flesh. Therefore what God has joined together, let not man separate" (Mark 10:5–9).

I have seen men and women try to defy these laws of relationships time and time again to their own destruction. Solomon wrote in Proverbs 18:1, "A man who isolates himself seeks his own desire; He rages against all wise judgment." This verse describes exactly what takes place when men and women become involved in affairs. They begin to isolate themselves from their families and all accountability relationships, and then they forsake, even resent, wise judgment. The result is faulty thinking based on false assumptions.

FALSE ASSUMPTIONS

The number of false assumptions that support this kind of behavior are legion, but a couple of them appear to be quite common. The *first false assumption* is that one can manage two relationships without violating either one. The *second false assumption* is that one can control the extramarital relationship and keep it from getting out of hand.

In an attempt to manage both relationships, the person will begin to compartmentalize his life. Trying to convince himself that his behavior is logical and therefore acceptable, he will place the two competing relationships in different categories. For example, a man might tell himself that one relationship is for love and family while the other is for friendship and sex. Now that they are separated and defined—no problem!

What is really amazing is to watch someone who is so deceived that he actually tries to sell his offended spouse on this line of thinking when he is caught: "Come on, honey, you've got to believe me. You're the one I love! It didn't mean anything. I promise. I love you. You're my wife." I must say, I've yet to see this approach go over well.

The other false assumption is that the extramarital relationship is manageable and will not progress past a certain point. For instance, Sam probably never intended for anything physical to come of the relationship with Karen. He just needed her support and her company. She gave him confidence because she valued his opinion. Likewise, Karen probably felt it was refreshing to be able to discuss spiritual things with a man she respected. He also listened to her. He actually cared about what concerned her. She hadn't felt cared for in quite some time, so what was the harm in that? They would soon find out.

CONSEQUENCES

It is rare that someone comes forward at this stage in the process, but the Holy Spirit does break through unexpectedly at times. Proverbs 18:19 states, "A brother offended is harder to win than a strong city." At this advanced stage, it is obvious that the oneness of the marital relationship is going to be dealt a severe blow. This is not a challenge any couple should attempt to tackle alone. They will need all the support and guidance they can get. The offended spouse's emotions go far beyond hurt and disappointment to a level more along the lines of betrayal and deep pain.

> The key to security will not merely be accountability, but the greatest security will arise out of true intimacy. True intimacy enables the offended spouse to be so in tune with the relationship that he or she can instantly sense emotional distance.

The recovery period will not be a short one and will require an incredible amount of effort, preferably under the guidance of a counselor. There will be a grieving process and some amount of paranoia along with legitimate fear and mistrust. The key to security will not merely be accountability, but the greatest security will arise out of true intimacy. True intimacy enables the offended spouse to be so in tune with the relationship that he or she can instantly sense emotional distance.

Obviously there will be repercussions involving the church as well. The person with whom the affair was developing will have her reputation and relationships negatively impacted.

As a pastor, one should expect to answer to the church leadership as they discuss the proper way to handle the situation. These meetings, with a touch of grace, will likely result in probation and/or possible mandatory leave contingent upon receiving counseling. Hopefully, the church will be mature enough not to panic by resorting to immediate termination. The church should set up an ongoing accountability structure that should have already been in place.

At this point the pastor may feel he is being punished in spite of the fact that he voluntarily confessed his sin. The truth is that even with a mature, gracious church, the pastor—by waiting this late in the process—has limited the options of those seeking to help.

By coming forward now, the pastor can perhaps keep his job. He has spared himself further failure and risk. The benefit of being honest at this stage is not in the correction he is experiencing but in all the consequences he will not experience by ending the relationship before further damage is done.

DAVID: A CASE STUDY
If it can happen to the best, it can happen to the rest.

"Then David sent messengers, and took her; and she came to him" (2 Sam. 11:4a).

David's inquiry revealed the identity of his fantasy woman. She was the wife of one of David's mighty men, Uriah the Hittite (2 Sam. 23:39). This meant she would be alone for an extended period of time, since her husband was at the battlefront.

I wonder how this anointed man, who usually sought God's blessing and direction, rationalized continuing further down the path of temptation. Could he have told himself something along these lines: *I'll just invite her up for dinner and conversation. There's no harm done.* Or perhaps he thought: *I'm the king and I should have what I desire. I deserve a woman of such beauty.*

> The benefit of being honest at this stage is not in the correction he is experiencing but in all the consequences he will not experience by ending the relationship before further damage is done.

The power of self-deception has a man almost blinded by this point. All he knows is what he wants. He is blind to responsibility, the feelings of others, and the impending consequences.

PILLAR PAGE

"God is faithful, who will not allow you to be tempted beyond what you are able . . . but . . . will also make the way of escape" (1 Cor. 10:13).

Prayer: "Lord, give me the courage to be honest and to obey you by choosing your way of escape. Amen."

❑ What are some ways you may have noticed that the relationship has intensified as sin matured?

❑ How has Sam's behavior changed in order to accommodate this relationship?

❏ How do Sam and Angela justify their thinking that their behavior is still in the safe range?

❏ Have you ever witnessed a similar scenario in the life of another minister? Did anyone try to warn him? How did he respond?

❏ Do you agree that ministers may be in a higher risk climate for affairs than many or most other professions?

❏ Have you ever considered how relationships develop? Do you think if you applied the principles of the four building blocks of intimacy and three laws of relationships to your marriage that you could improve your marital relationship? Maybe even rekindle a little romance?

CHAPTER 8

Sin Manifests
(Phase 5 of Temptation)

"Sin, when it is full-grown, brings forth death" (James 1:15).

"Mrs. Sanders, what kind of church do you go to that you stay until eleven o'clock at night?" Juanita blurted out as Karen walked through the door. "I thought nine-thirty and ten was bad enough, but eleven o'clock!"

Karen began her apology, "You're right to be upset, Ms. Juanita. It shouldn't happen again. These were just some unique circumstances. The other late hours should taper off as well after the seventy-fifth anniversary next month. Thank you for watching the children. I know they're safe with you here."

Karen accompanied Juanita to her car and thanked her again as she shut the car door. Juanita's car roared to life, and Karen watched the back of her baby-sitter's car

> **Characteristics of Phase 5:**
> In this phase the subtle compromises become blatant transgressions. The persons being tempted become more rebellious and feel justified in their choice. The two are completely blind to the consequences that are soon to follow, increasingly careless about hiding their sin, and consumed by their insatiable appetite for their sin of choice.

swing into the deserted street and the headlights take focus on the road as tears began to stream down her face.

She backed up a couple of steps and sat down. She began to feel her emotions well up within her so she ran into the house, moved quickly down the hall, and threw herself on the bed as she began to weep uncontrollably. *Thank God, Stewart's on the road,* she thought. *I've got a couple of days to pull myself together. It's not real. It'll never happen again. It can't. This is wrong! I can't do this.*

Her mind continued to race. *I can't be falling in love with Sam. He's my pastor. How can I face him? What will I do? I can't resign from everything because everyone will know something's up, something's wrong. Maybe we can pretend this never happened and just move on. Surely it won't happen again.*

Meanwhile, Sam was pacing back and forth in his office. He was also distraught. He knew they had crossed a line they had flirted with on a few occasions. This was big. This was trouble. This was wrong. *What do I do?* His thoughts raced with each change of direction as he continued to pace.

I'll call Karen and talk this out. No, I can't talk to her; there's been enough damage tonight. She probably wouldn't answer the phone anyway. His mind continued to race. *I should go home; it's so late, but I can't bring myself to face Angela if she's still up.*

I can't believe I kissed her . . . or did she kiss me? I'm not sure. But it didn't matter after the first kiss, because they both embraced, and passions roared to life for the next thirty or forty minutes. It was as if all the pent-up thoughts and feelings of several weeks unleashed themselves in one uncontrollable moment. Sam was still pondering the moment in disbelief. Conflicting feelings began to flood his soul. He was afraid, shocked, and ashamed on one hand, but on the other hand he felt exhilaration, passion, and strength—he felt like a man. *She wanted me,* he thought. *I know it's wrong, but she wanted me. STOP! I can't think like that!*

"God, what have I done? I've defiled your calling on my life. Lord, I know I've let busy-ness cause my time with you to slip, but you've got to help me. I feel like I've been in a desert for so long. Where are you? I can't do this!" With that cry for help, Sam turned out the lights, locked up the church, and headed home.

Karen and Sam avoided each other and made no contact for a little over a week, but they both knew they would eventually have to talk. So on one of the usual nights when they used to talk over coffee, after everyone had left, Sam stayed late in hopes Karen would stop by—and she did.

At first they apologized to each other, and they tried to draw a line in the sand just to be good friends. But Sam had not felt respected or wanted for a long time, and Angela seemed unresponsive. Karen was so lonely, and she did not feel valued or listened to by her husband. That would not be the last inappropriate encounter for Sam and Karen. They were both too needy, and they had too much freedom.

Sam had all the reasons he needed for missing blocks of time, and Karen's husband was on the road a lot. Besides, Karen was suspicious that her husband might be seeing someone in another town. He had done it once before. As long as she was home around ten o'clock, the baby-sitter didn't ask any questions.

Soon they found themselves in each other's arms again. Now they resigned themselves to the reality, and they became craftier to make their rendezvous less predictable. Sam found new ways to stealthily make his way to Karen's house in the afternoon for an extended lunch hour.

Angela noticed Sam's elevated mood and the extra spring in his step, but she assumed it was excitement about the seventy-fifth anniversary celebration that was now only a couple of weeks away. She figured Sam was just excited to have Mr. Torrence off his back for a while. Everyone was distracted. It was like Christmas around the church.

DANGER: STEEP GRADE AHEAD

Now the relationship has fully matured, and sin has manifested itself in the alluring realm of the hidden and the forbidden with no one to intervene. Proverbs 9:17–18 reveals, "Stolen water is sweet, and bread eaten in secret is pleasant. But he does not know that the dead are there." Under these conditions it was only a matter of time before the relationship became physical. Since relationships are meant to evolve, there was nowhere else for this relationship to go, as Sam and Karen now realized.

> **Proverbs 9:17–18 reveals, "Stolen water is sweet, and bread eaten in secret is pleasant. But he does not know that the dead are there."**

The relationship is well underway to becoming unmanageable. It's like Sam and Karen are on a runaway train, a relationship train, approaching a steep downhill grade with the hydraulic brakes leaking fluid.

Sam and Karen were startled at first by the sudden increase in speed, but they adjusted to what had happened, thinking they could regain control. The relationship train is yet to reach the steepest grade stretching down the mountainside toward the valley. They don't anticipate the sharp turns ahead, so Sam and Karen find the increased speed, the forbidden rush, exhilarating.

They have very little knowledge about how steep this downhill grade will be and how unmanageable this relationship train will become at its increasingly high rate of speed.

A runaway train racing toward its tragic end best relates the dynamics created by a relationship of this nature. There is no longer an easy escape out of the situation, and if they ride the train to the end, there is nothing ahead but destruction.

LEGITIMIZING SIN

After the infatuation starts to fade, just after the lust is satisfied, the forbidden couple will begin to realize the gravity of the situation. They will attempt to think of ways to legitimize the relationship. They may be weighing the cost of divorcing their spouses and marrying each other.

This is possibly what David was attempting to accomplish when he had Uriah killed. After all, this was sort of how it worked with Abigail. David was impressed with Abigail. When Nabal died, David was able to legitimately obtain Abigail as his wife. Only this time David violated an active marriage covenant, and he decided to play God by ending Uriah's life.

> It seems as though they have convinced themselves they would not be in the predicament if it were not for the failures of the noncheating spouse.

Another common way to justify or legitimize the illicit relationship is to demonize one's spouse in an attempt to pass the blame for the affair. At this point, the cheating spouse will criticize everything and become angry and accusatory without a moment's notice. It seems as though they have convinced themselves they would not be in the predicament if it were not for the failures of the non-cheating spouse.

Jesus taught us that men cannot honor two competing loyalties in his statement, "He will despise one and love the other."

The turmoil within the heart and mind of the wayward spouse is understandable when we consider what Paul has to say concerning slavery to sin:

> Therefore do not let sin reign in your mortal body, that you should obey it in its lusts. And do not present your members as instruments of unrighteousness to sin . . . Do you not know that to whom you present yourselves slaves to obey, you are that one's slaves whom you obey, whether of sin leading to death, or of obedience leading to righteousness? (Rom. 6:12–13, 16).

Sam and Karen have deceived themselves into choosing slavery to sin unto death.

Consequences

Death is the most accurate word one can use to describe the impact of adultery on a marriage and a ministry. Even if the marriage is somehow salvaged, the relationship will experience death to innocence and integrity, death to oneness, and death to the pastoral relationship with the community. The seeds of death have been sown, but death's full impact will not be known until the illicit relationship is unveiled. When it is unveiled—and it will be—then death will spread into every aspect of Sam and Karen's lives. We know this relationship will be exposed because both God and Satan have a vested interest in the truth.

God needs truth to be upheld in order to protect the purity of his church and to discipline these wayward children whom he loves. If a man or woman can continue in affairs without somehow being exposed, then I would check my spiritual birth record: "If you endure chastening, God deals with you as with sons; for what son is there whom a father does not chasten? But if you are without chastening, of which all have become partakers, then you are illegitimate and not sons" (Heb. 12:7–8).

Satan will also seek to expose the truth in order to exploit it and twist it. Satan's goal is to give God's enemies a reason to blaspheme the name of God, his church, and his messengers.

At this point, it may seem impossible to do the right thing by personally exposing this moral failure through the appropriate channels of authority and support. This is the last vestige of integrity that you can call forth on your own.

There will still be the consequences of death because sin has already been sown in the relationships. One's ministry as it exists will probably experience death, but we do serve a God of mercy. People will likely extend mercy to those who find the courage to reveal their own sin and seek help.

We also serve the God of resurrection power, who is able to raise marriages and ministries out of the grave. God is in the business of resurrecting the dead when people repent, submit to authority, and seek his healing.

DAVID: A CASE STUDY

If it can happen to the best, it can happen to the rest.

"And he slept with her . . . Then she went back home. The woman conceived and sent word to David, saying, 'I am pregnant'" (2 Sam. 11:4b–5 NIV).

Whatever David was thinking, it didn't matter once Bathsheba arrived at his house. I'm sure that the fantasies in David's mind had completely blinded him with passion and lust. Magnified by the forbidden nature and the secrecy of the encounter, it is likely that David found his momentary escape from the boredom, the apathy, or the depression in the excitement of the hunt.

Sin immediately manifests itself in every way from the sexual encounter to the conception of a child. Sin's conquest was complete, defiling the king and a soldier's marriage.

> People will likely extend mercy to those who find the courage to reveal their own sin and seek help.

Now that sin had become manifest, it began to multiply. More lies were told. Deception increased, involving all those in David's household. Corruption of others was inevitable: every servant who followed the king's orders became part of the web of secrecy, such as Joab and those underneath his command, who became accomplices in the murder of an innocent man.

Sin always makes life more and more complex, and it *always destroys innocence*. When sin becomes manifest, what once seemed to be the solution to our stress soon becomes its greatest source. The situation that we have created then begins to crush us. "When I kept silent, my bones wasted away through my groaning all day long. For day and night your hand was heavy upon me; my strength was sapped as in the heat of summer" (Ps. 32:3–4 NIV).

Pillar Page

"God is faithful, who will not allow you to be tempted beyond what you are able . . . but . . . will also make the way of escape" (1 Cor. 10:13).

Prayer: "Lord, give me the courage to be honest and to obey you by choosing your way of escape. Amen."

❏ Why do you think Sam and Karen were surprised when the relationship became physical?

❏ In what ways did they continue to deceive themselves?

❏ When temptation has progressed this far, how would you recommend they seek help?

❏ Do you know of a pastor who sought out assistance before his affair was exposed? How did the church respond?

❏ Do you know of a couple who salvaged a healthy relationship after an affair? Have you ever thought to ask them how they did it?

CHAPTER 9

Exposure—Discovery and Consequences (Phase 6 of Temptation)

"Sin . . . brings forth death" (James 1:15).

The seventy-fifth anniversary celebration of First Church of Sand City was a huge success. Seven former pastors came in from out of town. Reverend Roberts, against whom all the other min-

> **Characteristics of Phase 6:**
> This phase is characterized by confrontation when what was done in secret is made known.

isters had the unpleasant experience of being measured, brought the message. The senior adults were ecstatic to hear Reverend Roberts in their pulpit again after so many years.

The church had a video presentation composed of pictures that depicted the seventy-five years of ministry by generations of First Church families. Pictures had been collected from the congregation for weeks, and the editing of the video took days.

The congregation had dinner on the ground and special music by a variety of soloists, instrumentalists, and quartets. It was a big day for the children as well, with games and contests and plenty of treats and prizes. There were balloons and streamers and plenty of excitement. The day was a complete success, and everyone was singing Karen's praises for all her hard work. Mr. Torrence even complimented Sam for his leadership.

Sadly, though, the season of victory and celebration would be short-lived. In less than a week, the church would be cast into the depths of scandal.

The Wednesday after the celebration, Karen scheduled a meeting for her planning committee to evaluate the event and to tie up loose ends. Everyone was in good spirits, but still exhausted. As a result, their meeting was shorter than usual. The choir also had an abbreviated practice so everyone could rest up and get back into a routine.

Like many times before, Karen found things to do until everyone left the church. *Sam and I can have some extra time and I can still get home fairly early*, she thought to herself. Karen and Sam had discussed trying to distance themselves and work on their marriages. While their physical and emotional feelings for each other were incredibly strong, they still knew it was wrong, and they both had children to think about as well as their spouses. They also realized that without the big event schedule, there would be a greater risk of being discovered. This would be the obvious time to try to make a clean break. Karen eventually made her way to the church office, and as usual, the church was deserted. She used the key she had obtained as chairman of the celebration committee to open and then lock behind her the back door to the offices.

I don't want this to be any harder than it has to be. Our conversation needs to be short, the good-bye sweet, and the finality secured, she thought as she made her way to Sam's office. As she entered the office, it felt a little awkward. They both stood there, not knowing what to say.

"Oh, Sam," she said, with a crack in her voice. They embraced as though they were never going to see each other again, and they kissed with such passion it was like he was going off to war.

At Karen's house, Juanita heard the garage door open. *That's strange; Mr. Sanders isn't due in town until tomorrow, according to Karen.*

Noticing Karen's car wasn't in the garage, Stewart's first words were not, "Hello, Juanita!" but, "Where's Karen?"

"Why, she's still at her committee meeting at the church, I would assume," Juanita replied.

"I came by the church on the way home, but the car I saw wasn't Karen's."

A look of concern came over his face, and he began to turn a little red. "Juanita, would you please stay a little longer while I try to locate Karen?" Stewart asked, as he stormed out the door, not waiting for an answer.

Stewart's car expressed its driver's frustration as its wheels spun rapidly in reverse, throwing gravel against the undercarriage of the car. Stewart sped toward the church, not caring if he got a ticket. If what his jealous gut was telling him was true, he would make the police follow him and, after they wrote him a ticket, they could help him search the church.

When Stewart reached the church, the car that he assumed was the pastor's was still parked in the same place, but there was no sign of Karen's car. Stewart slowly circled the church hoping he was mistaken, and, as he made his way around to the back of the church, he spotted Karen's car parked less noticeably in the corner lot.

It was a cloudy night with low floating clouds that made an eerie picture in the moonlight. But this was nothing compared to the storm brewing inside Stewart. He parked his car, not bothering to park it according to the lines. He wound his way around the church checking the doors, but the ones he checked were locked. Many of the lights were still on, so a door had to be open somewhere.

I'm a fool, Stewart said to himself. *I've had bad feelings about all those planning meetings for some time now, but I thought: Not Karen, maybe someone else, but not Karen.*

As Stewart turned the corner to cross the backyard of the church, he could see the dew and the water standing on the grass, reflecting the light of the moon and a nearby street lamp. He could smell the fresh cut grass and see the clippings building on his shoes as he tried to watch his step. Then he looked up and stopped dead in his tracks. The only window to the pastor's office faced the backyard of the church. The shade was pulled down, but a silhouette could be seen—two people obviously entwined, two shadows becoming one in a forbidden embrace.

Stewart turned on the spot and hastily made his way back to the car. He didn't have his cell phone—his battery was low, so he had taken it into the house with his luggage to charge for the next day. He shut the door and sped back to the house in half the time the first leg of the trip had taken.

He rushed in with a bang, and a cold breeze filled the room. Juanita was startled and the words, "You'll wake the children," blurted out of her mouth.

Stewart gave no reply. He stormed straight into the kitchen, picked up the church directory from the counter, and began thumbing through the pages with careless haste.

"Is there a problem? Is Karen OK? Has there been. . . ?"

Stewart turned with his face red and nostrils flaring. "So do you know what that slut I called my wife has been doing the last few months while you watched our kids? She's been doing the pastor, that's what!"

The shocked look and Juanita's gasp communicated that she had no idea. "I think I need to go now, Stewart, unless you need me for the kids."

"No, I'm not going anywhere," Stewart replied.

Juanita backed out the door as she picked up her purse and pulled the door closed.

Stewart finally found the page with the staff names and numbers. Sam's name was at the top of the page and the number for the chairman of the deacons, Mr. Torrence, was at the bottom. Stewart picked up the phone and began to dial.

Angela had just put Sara to bed, and gotten Jon partially to bed, and Tommy had just finished his homework when the phone began to ring. Angela hurried through the house to the study where she picked up the phone with an out-of-breath "Hello."

She was greeted by a rude, mean voice on the other end of the line, "Lady, do you know where your husband is?"

"At the church, I suppose," she answered, caught off guard.

"That's right," the angry voice replied, "with my wife—alone!" And he slammed down the phone. Stewart's eyes fell to the bottom of the page noticing the title, *chairman of deacons*.

Angela yelled back to Tommy, "I need to step out for a few minutes. I won't be long. You and Jon go ahead and get to bed. If you need anything, call Ms. Doris next door." Before any questions could be asked, she grabbed Sam's spare set of keys and was out the door. She made the usual twenty-minute trip in ten, and her headlights flashed against the side of Sam's car as she pulled into the parking lot.

The Confrontation

Sam and Karen were just about to convince themselves to pull away when they heard a key turn in the door. They were no more than a foot apart when Angela stepped through the door. Sam and Karen stood there stunned, frozen in time, and guilty. Angela's eyes filled with tears as she cursed Sam and swept all the trinkets off a nearby end table. "How could you!" she shouted. "Four years of seminary, one struggling church after another, and the kids! You fool!" She cursed Sam again and left almost as quickly as she had appeared.

Karen turned away, no longer able to face Sam. "My God, what have we done?" she said as she slowly walked out in the manner she had intended an hour earlier—oh, how she wished she had; with all of her being, she wished she had.

When Karen got to the car, she called home. When she heard Stewart's voice, she knew what had happened. She said, "I'm not coming home tonight," and she turned off her phone. As she drove away, she headed toward her hairdresser's, who was also a close friend, and asked to stay the night.

Unexpected Grace

Sam was picking up the last of the mess Angela had made when he looked up to see Mr. Torrence standing in the door. Sam stood to his feet and walked back to his desk to create some distance. He couldn't face Mr. Torrence, so he opened the shades to look out the window. Mr. Torrence decided to break the silence, "Sam, I know you know why I'm here. I'm really sad to see this happen. I know I'm a crusty old man, but I was actually beginning to warm up to you.

"This is a big mess, and there will have to be a deacon's meeting tomorrow night. Of course, you know you'll have to resign. I'll make sure you get at least three months' severance pay." Sam glanced up appreciatively as Mr. Torrence continued, "Come to think about it, didn't you manage a restaurant once? That means you know how to handle money. If you're interested, I'll call one of my friends at one of the banks in a nearby town. You could work there as a teller while you try to work on your marriage and figure out where to go from here."

Sam continued to stare out the window with tears running down his face and a pit in his stomach, but he managed to croak out a response, "Thanks, Bill. I wouldn't have expected that . . ."

"What . . . from a calloused old man like me?" Bill interrupted. "You're right. I throw my weight around too much, and I shouldn't be so hard on you young preachers. I just like to ask the hard questions and test your metal, but I'm not your enemy. I've seen a lot in my lifetime, son, and I don't want you to leave here without hope."

"Thank you," Sam replied.

"I would advise you to get anything you need so you don't have to come back to the church for a few days. I'll call the associational director and get us a preacher for Sunday. Let's see, this is Wednesday; the deacons will meet tomorrow night; you come by my house Friday morning, and I'll update you on what was decided. Sam, are you listening to me?"

"Yes, I am," Sam replied. "I'm grateful, but I don't deserve the help you're offering me."

"I know," said Bill, "but isn't that what the gospel message is all about? Son, you've got a bigger mess at home than you'll ever have to face here. It's probably going to get worse before it gets better, but you've got a young family to try and save. I suggest you go home and get started. I'll go around and turn off the lights while I pray for you. You get your things, and we'll leave together."

THE FALLOUT

When Sam got home, the house was dark and quiet. The door to the master bedroom was shut and Sam dared not open it. He looked in on the kids and began to cry. *They're so innocent*, he thought; *they don't deserve this*. Sam walked into the living room where he collapsed, begging for help and forgiveness.

"I don't want to lose everything, Lord, please help me. Please help Angela find it in her heart to give me another chance," he groaned. Exhausted, he eventually made his way onto the couch where he fell asleep.

The next few months would be months of shame, depression, anger, sadness, confusion, and loss. Karen and Stewart would go through a bitter divorce and move out of the community. Karen would have to begin rebuilding her life as a single parent and return to the workforce. The stress, turmoil, and regrets would leave Karen battling with bouts of depression.

Angela was angry and bitter, but she was willing to see if counseling might help. She knew that staying together was in the best interest of the children. But it was going to be a difficult trail of anger and tears before the relationship would have much to offer. Trust takes a long time to rebuild.

If it hadn't been for a visit from Mrs. Wilson, Angela probably would have filed for divorce. Years ago Mrs. Wilson's husband had violated their marriage of fifteen years. Mrs. Wilson told Angela that upon discovery of the affair she immediately filed for divorce. Mr. Wilson ended the affair, but Mrs. Wilson had refused to give him another chance. She felt justified in her anger for several years before she realized the negative impact her decision had made in the lives of her sons. Mrs. Wilson asked Angela to consider giving counseling a chance before making a final decision about the option of divorce.

Sam took the bank teller job that Mr. Torrence had arranged in the same town where they were getting counseling. The family had to move a forty-minute drive from Sand City, the boys had to change schools, and Angela had to get a part-time job to make ends meet. Now she not only had to work through her bitterness about the affair, but she had to deal with not being home with the children as much as before.

These were hard times, and they tried to shelter the children as much as they could. At times, though, Tommy's anger would get the best of him and he would get in trouble at school.

First Church of Sand City lost all the momentum gained by the seventy-fifth anniversary celebration. Mr. Torrence did his best to squelch the rumor mill and formed a committee to find a new pastor. However, church attendance continued to decline, and the congregation was becoming increasingly demoralized. Sin had run its course!

THERE IS NO SUCH THING AS SECRET SIN

Since the beginning of biblical history, men and women have been attempting unsuccessfully to hide their sin from God. In Genesis 3, Adam and Eve attempted to avoid exposure of their sin by hiding in the garden. Generations later, the sons of Jacob attempted to deceive their father about the disappearance of his youngest son Joseph, only to be exposed after several years.

> Since the beginning of biblical history, men and women have been attempting unsuccessfully to hide their sin from God.

In Joshua 7, Achan's sin of coveting was exposed, costing him his life, the lives of his family, and the destruction of everything he owned. Nathan's challenge to David in 2 Samuel 12 rings throughout history. He exposed David's sin about Uriah, the Hittite, and Bathsheba: "You are the man!" The Proverbs of Solomon, the second son of David and Bathsheba, would be replete with warnings about the exposure, shame, and consequences of adultery. Throughout the Old Testament, God's prophets and God's judgments are constantly bringing to light the hidden sins of God's chosen people. The New Testament begins with Jesus clearly warning his disciples about the inevitable exposure of sin:

> Beware of the leaven of the Pharisees, which is hypocrisy. For there is nothing covered that will not be revealed, nor hidden that will not be known. Therefore whatever you have spoken in the dark will be heard in the light, and what you have spoken in the ear in inner rooms will be proclaimed on the housetops. (Luke 12:1–3)

115

The apostle Paul, being inspired by God's Spirit, continues the theme of the certain exposure of sin: "In the day when God will judge the secrets of men by Jesus Christ" (Rom. 2:16). "So then each of us shall give account of himself to God" (Rom. 14:12). "Do not be deceived, God is not mocked; for whatever a man sows, that he will also reap" (Gal. 6:7). "Marriage is honorable among all, and the bed undefiled; but fornicators and adulterers God will judge" (Heb. 13:4).

> God has also made it clear that as certainly as secret sins will be exposed, consequences will also be incurred.

JUDGMENT GUARANTEED

God has also made it clear that as certainly as secret sins will be exposed, consequences will also be incurred. King Solomon, growing up in a household marked by the reproach of adultery, had much to say on the subject of the consequences of adultery:

> Remove your way far from her, and do not go near the door of her house, lest you give your honor to others, and your years to the cruel one; lest aliens be filled with your wealth, and your labors go to the house of a foreigner; and you mourn at last, when your flesh and body are consumed, and say: "How I have hated instruction, and my heart despised correction!" (Prov. 5:8–12)

Sam and Karen have now become the embodiment of these truths. In one moment of truth, the church's shining stars have become the community's fallen stars. The exposure was swift, sudden, and pervasive. They have no honor in the community, and they will relocate in shame.

Karen will lose years of investment in her community. Now she will have less support from her husband than she had before the affair, and she will have to rebuild in another community as a single parent.

Sam will lose the benefit of the years he and Angela sacrificed for his seminary education. At least for a period of time, he will have to regroup in another profession. Out of desperation, he will have to accept a job that does not acknowledge his experience and his education. He will spend several years in a job where he is overeducated and underpaid.

> Sam's wife and children will also bear the reproach of his moral failure. Angela will not only have to overcome the violation of the affair, but she will also have to work through the resentment.

Sam's wife and children will also bear the reproach of his moral failure. Angela will not only have to overcome the violation of the affair, but she will also have to work through the resentment of losing time with her children in order to return to the workplace. The boys will have to adjust to a new school and to child care, and little Sara will no longer spend the best part of her day with her mom.

GOD'S GRACE

When experiencing the judgment of the Lord because of your own guilt or your association with someone else's guilt, never fail to recognize the grace of God. For example, when God removed Adam and Eve from the Garden of Eden, he still covered their nakedness. Likewise, in Sam and Angela's case, Sam was removed from his ministry position and forced to take a lower-level job, but he was never unemployed.

Mr. Torrence, the man who appeared to be Sam's nemesis, became his greatest source of grace and support. God often reaches out to comfort us from the most unexpected places.

> **God often reaches out to comfort us from the most unexpected places.**

Thankfully, the Lord's discipline is only for a season. If we repent, in due time he will begin to restore the years that the locusts have eaten (Joel 2:25); he will restrain the destroyer (Exod. 12:23), and he will restore the joy of our salvation (Ps. 51:12). It gets worse before it gets better, but I have seen fallen brothers restored and new ministries arise out of ashes of failure. Ministries created to reach out to those overlooked and neglected by the mainstreams of Christian ministry.

King David expressed it best in Psalm 51:1–17:

> Have mercy upon me, O God, according to Your lovingkindness; according to the multitude of Your tender mercies, blot out my transgressions. Wash me thoroughly from my iniquity, and cleanse me from my sin. . . . Behold, You desire truth in the inward parts, and in the hidden part You will make me to know wisdom. Purge me . . . and I shall be clean; wash me, and I shall be whiter than snow. Make me hear joy and gladness, that the bones You have broken may rejoice. . . . Create in me a clean

> **It gets worse before it gets better, but I have seen fallen brothers restored and new ministries arise out of ashes of failure.**

heart, O God, and renew a steadfast spirit within me. Do not cast me away from Your presence, and do not take Your Holy Spirit from me. Restore to me the joy of Your salvation, and uphold me by Your generous Spirit. Then I will teach transgressors Your ways, and sinners shall be converted. . . . The sacrifices of God are a broken spirit, a broken and a contrite heart; these, O God, You will not despise.

It is believed that this is the psalm David wrote in his penitent response to Nathan's challenge over David's sin with Bathsheba.

David: A Case Study

If it can happen to the best, it can happen to the rest.

God told David that he would humble him before all Israel because of his indulgent pride: "Then Nathan said to David, 'You are the man!' . . . the sword shall never depart from your house . . . I will rise up adversity against you from your own house . . . I will take your wives . . . and give them to your neighbor, and he will lie with your wives . . . For you did it secretly, but I will do this thing before all Israel . . . the child also who is born to you shall surely die" (2 Sam. 12:7–14).

God's love for David was great, and God would later grant David forgiveness and a restored spiritual relationship, but there would still be the consequential judgments of sin to face. The thread of judgment would weave its way into every fabric of David's life until the day he went to rest with his fathers. Perhaps this is why Solomon wrote these words about a man caught in adultery: "Wounds and dishonor he will get, and his reproach will not be wiped away" (Prov. 6:33).

This reproach would open the door of sexual sin among David's children, only to be followed by violence and revenge. Exploitation and rebellion would run rampant through David's household. Just as Nathan prophesied, the sword would strike David's household again and again and again.

David's respect among his warriors must have also suffered irreparable harm. The king had betrayed one of his mighty men. While Uriah gave his life, David took his wife.

PILLAR PAGE

"God is faithful, who will not allow you to be tempted beyond what you are able . . . but . . . will also make the way of escape" (1 Cor. 10:13).

Prayer: "Lord, give me the courage to be honest and to obey you by choosing your way of escape. Amen."

❏ Have you ever experienced God's judgment and God's grace at the same time?

❏ Do you feel most churches handle this kind of situation well? How do you feel about Mr. Torrence's leadership in this situation?

❏ While the Scriptures may give Angela permission to divorce Sam, it does not mean she should feel she has to divorce. What do you think about her decision to stay with Sam?

❏ Do you know of any unique ministries that started as an effort to rebuild after a moral failure?

CHAPTER 10

Proper Perspective

A proper perspective implies a correct perception of reality. In reference to temptation and moral failure, a correct perception of reality is one that accepts the nature of our humanity, fears the judgment of God, acknowledges the schemes of the devil, and is comforted by the grace we receive through Jesus Christ.

In today's culture it seems the word *acceptance* has often come to mean "blind tolerance," with no sense of proper expectations or responsibilities. This concept is not what is intended in our discussion about accepting the nature of our humanity. The "acceptance" being proposed is that we think accurately and soberly about ourselves, understanding our own bent toward sin. We must recognize the appetites of our fleshly nature, the deceptive ability of our heart to accept the lies of Satan, and the potential distortions in our thinking. We also need to be aware of the thirst for righteousness and purity in our reborn spirit and the strength in our inner man through the Holy Spirit.

> We must not forget the power of a personal and loving God who will deliver and save us through his Son, Jesus Christ. This perspective allows us to walk with caution but not in fear.

Above all else, we must not forget the power of a personal and loving God who will deliver and save us through his Son, Jesus Christ. This perspective allows us to walk with caution but not in fear. When this perspective is in place, we are confident in the grace of God but consciously aware of his judgment should we choose to live foolishly.

Safe & Sound is written with the intention of helping the reader focus on the important balance of refusing to treat sin lightly (without slipping into paranoia) while pursuing personal holiness. Such a balance cannot be achieved without an awareness that we have an enemy seeking to subvert our course at every turn.

> **Satan's schemes are well executed, dangerous and deadly, but they are detectable or avoidable.**

We must always remember that the devil's greatest power is to scheme and to deceive. He wants to deceive us into thinking that if we become the target of enticement, we will be powerless to defend against its sudden, surprising onslaught. Satan's other strategy is just the opposite: to convince us that moral failure happens to other, weak-minded, less-committed people, but it is not likely to happen to us.

Both of these assumptions are blindingly false. The unfolding of Satan's plans sets us up for a fall. He has studied us and has uniquely prepared for us a tailor-made invitation to sin that will be attractive to our strengths as well as our weaknesses. Satan's schemes are well-executed, dangerous, and deadly, but they are detectable and avoidable.

Thanks to Jesus' gift of the Holy Spirit who lives in us, we will always be provided a way of escape because greater is he who lives in us than he who is in the world. Since temptation and enticement require a series of poor choices, there is usually more than one opportunity to escape. If we choose to flee youthful lusts, as Paul recommended to Timothy, then we will be greatly rewarded for our obedience.

Jesus said that his Spirit would enable us to know the truth and that the truth would set us free. Because of the power of the Holy Spirit, lies and deception have no power against us unless we allow it. We may choose to ignore God's warnings and indulge. If we make that choice, the consequences will be more pervasive than we could ever anticipate. Whether we admit it or not, we are making the choice between freedom and slavery, between God and man.

> Since temptation and enticement require a series of poor choices, there is usually more than one opportunity to escape.

Finally, we must walk daily in the comfort we have in knowing that we live in the presence of a gracious God who perfectly balances judgment and loving-kindness. Even when we have chosen poorly, God is there to help us rebuild when we choose to repent and return to him. The reproach of moral failure may leave a lasting stamp on our earthly lives, but it is not the final word, and it does not disqualify us from future blessings. If we humble ourselves under the mighty hand of God, drawing near to him, he will draw near to us. Our God and Lord Jesus Christ has taught us time and time again that his arm is not too short that he cannot save. He will hear our cries and save us.

Therefore, having a proper perspective with reference to present realities and future glories, let us remember who we are. In the words of the apostle Paul,

For you were once darkness, but now you are light in the Lord. Walk as children of light . . . finding out what is acceptable to the Lord. And have no fellowship with the unfruitful works of darkness, but rather expose them . . . See then that you walk circumspectly, not as fools, but as wise, redeeming the time, because the days are evil. Therefore do not be unwise, but understand what the will of God is. (Eph. 5:8–11, 15–17)

PROPER RESPONSE

If we have a proper perspective, understanding the human condition and spiritual realities, what should our proper response be? Who better to give us our answer than Solomon, who grew up in a household that had experienced the reproach of adultery, and a man who asked God for wisdom?

The answer that Solomon wrote as a proper response to avoid adultery is found in Proverbs 4:23–27:

Keep your heart with all diligence, for out of it spring the issues of life. Put away from you a deceitful mouth, and put perverse lips far from you. Let your eyes look straight ahead, and your eyelids look right before you. Ponder the path of your feet, and let all your ways be established. Do not turn to the right or the left; remove your foot from evil.

GUARD YOUR HEART

Proverbs 4:23 admonishes us to "keep" (guard) our hearts with diligence. Solomon teaches that we are to guard our hearts because out of the heart flow the "issues of life." What is meant by our "heart"? How do we guard the precious treasure of the heart?

The principle issues of life are our love relationships: our relationships with God, our spouse, and ourselves. When we guard our heart, we guard these relationships.

The Hebrew term translated as "heart" in Proverbs 4:23 is *leb* or *lebab*. The word is sometimes translated as "mind"; at other times it is considered to imply strength of feeling, or it may be used to refer to a choice of the will. By

> He calls our attention to three critical areas that are in need of great discipline. We must guard what we say, what we see, and where we go.

this we can conclude that when we are guarding our hearts, we are protecting our most precious relationships in life by keeping our minds pure, our emotions in check, and our wills in line with God's. These are the benefits of guarding the heart.

Solomon not only exhorts us to guard our hearts (mind, will, and emotions), but he also gives practical advice on how to accomplish this task. He calls our attention to three critical areas that are in need of great discipline. We must guard what we say, what we see, and where we go.

Our speech is critical to healthy relationships. This is why Paul wrote in Ephesians 4:29, "Let no corrupt word proceed out of your mouth, but what is good for necessary edification [building up], that it may impart grace to the hearers." Corrupt communication in our Proverbs passage would be words of deceit or untruth or perverse words meant to mislead.

If you wish to guard your heart against temptation, you will need to monitor your communication with God, your spouse, and yourself. Jesus taught that our communication reveals the content of our hearts. Healthy hearts have healthy relationships, and healthy relationships have healthy communication. The following are characteristics of healthy communication:

- a constant flow of information
- regular interaction
- the words are pleasant and positive
- when the topic is negative, the words are still respectful
- communication is welcomed
- the truth is freely spoken
- thoughts of gratitude, appreciation, and acceptance are conveyed
- encouragement is freely given

When we yield to temptation, our communication is the first to change:

- the flow of information becomes infrequent
- interaction becomes inconsistent and defensive
- words become unpleasant and manipulative
- our words demonstrate a lack of respect
- communication is forced
- our words become deceptive and convey half-truths, and
- our thoughts convey the negatives of our relationship as our discontent increases

If you wish to guard your heart, monitor your communication. The time and quality of your conversations with God and your spouse will change for the positive if your relationship is growing stronger. It will reflect the negative if the relationship is growing weaker. How we speak to each other has a lot to do with how we feel about God, our spouses, and ourselves.

Solomon emphasized the importance of monitoring the objects of our gaze with the same intensity with which he warned us about our communication. Jesus also emphasized the importance of our eyes in Matthew 6:22–23, suggesting that what we gaze upon determines the ratio of light and darkness in our soul. The purity of our gaze seems to have a direct correlation with the purity of our mind. Much of what we covet begins first with the lust of the eyes.

This is why it is imperative that we be aware of how we are affected when we see certain people. There are some people who, in our eyes, awaken desire. There is something about them that appeals to us—the way they dress, the way they carry themselves, their natural beauty, or some other quality. We need to avoid being alone with these people or in close contact with them at all costs. Whenever possible, send someone else to interact with that person.

Another issue of great concern is pornography. The Internet has made this enemy of the heart more accessible than ever. In a recent publication of *Unchained,* the magazine of Pure Life Ministries, some startling statistics were revealed. Steve Gallagher, in his article entitled "The Greatest Threat to the Church Today," shared this unsettling news: "According to Promise Keepers, 65% of the men responding to a poll they took indicated they have a struggle with pornography" (winter 2002, p. 4).

Pornography makes everyone an easy target for our spiritual adversary. Pornography creates an appetite that cannot be filled.

The more you feed it, the more you need it. Our spouses cannot possibly live up to our fantasies, nor should they attempt to do so. A lust-controlled person becomes a discontented, uncommunicative, selfish simpleton who is incapable of a mature, honest, intimate relationship based in reality.

We must be diligent to monitor the purity of our thoughts. If we find ourselves having difficulty being honest with ourselves about the condition of our thought lives, then we should do the following exercise:

- List the magazines and articles you read or to which you subscribe and the Web sites you visit regularly.
- List the movies you rent and the cable channels you watch.
- List the number of people who regularly cross your path that awaken desire.
- List anyone you obsess about intimately (emotionally or sexually) besides your spouse.
- List the recurring discontented thoughts (emotionally or sexually) you have about your spouse.

This information should reveal to you the condition of your mind and the importance of monitoring what you see and think. This will underscore the importance of Paul's teaching that Christians should be "bringing every thought into captivity to the obedience of Christ" (2 Cor. 10:5).

Finally, if we monitor where we go as well as what we say and what we see, then high-risk situations will be greatly reduced. One of the signs of being enticed is when we begin to think of ways to be near someone. When we change the course of our lives, we change the experiences of our lives.

In Proverbs 4:27, Solomon warns us to "remove" our foot from evil. In 2 Timothy 2:22, Paul says to "flee" youthful lusts. In the Book of James we are told to "resist the devil" (James 4:7). So the question is: When it comes to temptation, do we resist or do we flee?

When the devil attacks our courage or our faith, we should resist him and stand firm. If, on the other hand, he chooses to entice us with the alluring qualities of the opposite sex, then we are to flee as fast and as far away from the situation as we possibly can.

Proverbs 4:23–27 is a wealth of practical knowledge on how to respond to temptation. Put Solomon's advice into practice, and your marriage and your ministry should finish the race intact—safe and sound.

Appendix I

Dealing with Temptations

"God is faithful, who will not allow you to be tempted beyond what you are able . . . but . . . will also make the way of escape" (1 Cor. 10:13).

What are the secrets in your life that Satan uses to blackmail you into self-pity?

_____

_____

_____

_____

You can know you have entered into self-pity thinking by paying attention to your thoughts of injustice:

- *I deserve more respect, and my spouse will never give me that respect.*
- *No one should have to do without the love and affection I'm missing in this marriage.*

- *She's/he's obviously not going to give me the love and attention I need, so I guess I'll have to get it some other way.*

Have you told yourself statements like these?

What are some of the statements you make to yourself to help justify compromising behavior?

_____

_____

_____

_____

What are the lies spoken into your thoughts to convince you to struggle alone?

- *No one will understand.*
- *If anyone knew about this, they would be disgusted with me.*
- *If you tell anyone this is a problem, they'll never respect you again.*
- *If you tell anyone about this, you'll be fired for sure.*
- *No one will love you if they know the truth about you.*

- Others: _____

_____

_____

_____

_____

_____

If you have not completed the process of choosing lifeguards (accountability partners) for your life and ministry, please refer to chapter 5 and complete the Pillar Page.

Assuming that you have lifeguards in place, the following information should be shared with them:

- Who is this high-risk person?
- What is the nature of your relationship?
- How long have you known this person?
- When did the nature of your relationship begin to change?
- Do you think the attraction is mutual?
- How many different ways is this person involved in your life?
- Is your spouse aware of this situation in any way?

What inappropriate overtures have you made toward this person to this point (even if the inappropriateness is only motive)?

_____

_____

_____

_____

What steps have you taken on your own to resist this attraction?

_____

_____

_____

_____

In what ways has your obsession or attraction to this person intensified?

_____

_____

_____

_____

In what ways can you limit your exposure to this person?

_____

_____

_____

In what ways is your exposure to this person unavoidable?

_____

_____

_____

_____

Is a transfer or dismissal possible?

_____

_____

_____

_____

Accountability often breaks the power of temptation because temptation is powered by secrecy.

Set proper boundaries—personal policies for managing ministry relationships. The following are a few examples:

❑ When counseling with the opposite sex, you might stay in a place visible to your secretary but far enough away so that she can't hear.

❑ You may determine to counsel someone of the opposite sex no more than three times, then to follow a referral plan.

❑ Avoid situations that isolate you and the opposite sex.

❑ Check working relationships with the opposite sex with your spouse and make sure they do not feel threatened.

Appendix II

Digging Deeper

List any obvious deficits you can identify in your childhood and adolescent experience:

- *Emotional Deficit* (lack of acceptance, lack of expressions of love, lack of safety from cruel criticism, anger, or embarrassment, lack of attention)

_____

_____

_____

_____

- *Intellectual Deficit* (your thoughts and ideas were never considered, you were rarely listened to, your ideas were usually rejected and ridiculed)

_____

_____

_____

_____

- *Physical Deficit* (fear of physical harm, lack of security in the home due to family or strangers, constant changes of residence, neglect of health issues, misuse of family resources, such as rent money gambled away)

_____

_____

_____

- *Spiritual Deficit* (lack of safety in the home makes it difficult to trust God, God's rules were used for manipulation and control, extreme hypocrisy displayed by the adults)

_____

_____

_____

_____

The deficits described above are the missing puzzle pieces that create the needs, fears, and behaviors that sabotage relationships.

Core Needs: My top five needs that I hope to receive from my marriage. (Circle your top five needs in this list or create your own under "other.")

Affection

Appreciation

Intimacy

Recreational partner

Financial security

Sexual fulfillment

Sense of belonging

Comfortable home

Respect

Friendship

Acceptance

Emotional

Other: _____

_____

Resulting Fears: (Sample statements revealing fear: "I'm most afraid that I will not be protected. I am afraid you will leave me like my dad left my mom.")

1._____

_____

_____

_____

2._____

_____

_____

_____

_____

3._____

_____

_____

_____

_____

4._____

_____

_____

_____

_____

Resulting Behaviors: ("When I sense I'm going to be criticized, I attack first.")

1._____

_____

_____

_____

_____

2._____

_____

_____

_____

3._____

_____

_____

_____

_____

4._____

_____

_____

_____

Before completing the rest of this exercise, consider the following suggestions:

- Start with the simplest request for change first.
- You can reuse the format of these questions to fine-tune your marriage in the future with more difficult challenges.
- Make sure you can share these requests without fighting or emotionally wounding each other. (If you can't, seek professional counseling.)
- Read each other's sheets once for facts and then a second time for feelings.
- Discuss your sheets by taking turns speaking and listening. Do not interrupt to counter or defend yourself. Wait your turn.
- Choose a need, fear, or behavior to focus on each week.

Name two practical ways your spouse can better meet your core needs. (Example: "Call me when you're going to be late so I will know you value my feelings and my time.")

1._____

_____

_____

_____

_____

2._____

_____

_____

_____

Name two specific ways your spouse can assist you in calming your fears. ("Stop threatening to divorce me when we argue.")

1._____

_____

_____

_____

2._____

_____

_____

_____

_____

Talk together about specific ways you might attempt to better control negative behaviors in the future. ("When I'm tempted to get angry, I will sit down, take a deep breath, and think about my words before I speak.")

1._____

_____

_____

_____

_____

2._____

_____

_____

_____

_____

3._____

_____

_____

_____

_____

Set aside time to consistently be together and keep communication open so that sharing is casual and consistent, rather than intense and inconsistent.

Appendix III

Helpful Advice for the Wounded Spouse

Jesus was quite clear in his statements about marriage and divorce concerning sexual immorality as a legitimate cause for ending a marriage (Matt. 19:7–9). But Jesus was stating that divorce was permissible, not necessarily advisable. The offended spouse does not have to feel compelled to seek a divorce if he or she wishes to give the marriage another chance.

This decision needs to be made cautiously with much prayer and counsel. Wisdom is to avoid basing the decision on the offense alone. One will want to take into consideration the willingness of the wayward spouse to take proper action and not his or her affinity for merely making promises.

When the marriage has been violated, it is natural for the wounded spouse to attempt to shield the children from the infidelity. It is also common to attempt to spare the children the trauma of divorce as well. When this is the case, the wounded spouse feels her hands are tied and she has little or no power to demand change. A common mistake at this point is to beg and plead for the wayward spouse to end the affair, which rarely has the desired result.

Knowledge of the affair and possible divorce are not the only traumas confronting the children. It is no less traumatic for the children to witness one parent continually dishonoring the other. What are we teaching our children about marriage? Do you want to teach them that when they get married, they no longer have any rights to protect themselves?

A healthier response to this situation is to realize that the decision to save the marriage is in the hands of the wayward spouse. The decision is his, but you set the conditions. Mandatory counseling and an immediate end to the competing relationship are a good beginning.

When an affair comes to light, seek the counsel of a Christian marriage counselor immediately. This counselor should be able to guide you on how you can set boundaries. **Boundaries are the properly communicated expectations that enable us to protect ourselves and our children, while placing the responsibility of honoring the marriage back on the shoulders of the wayward spouse.**

This enables the wounded spouse to force the wayward spouse to take responsibility for decisions about the future of the marriage. Proper boundaries enable us to say, "I'm committed to a lasting marriage, but I refuse to be dishonored in this relationship. My choice has been made; the final decision is now yours. You will either end the other relationship immediately and permanently and we will seek marriage counseling, or else you are telling me that you have chosen the other relationship over our marriage."

Appendix IV

Stress in Marriage and Ministry

"Come to Me, all you who labor and are heavy laden, and I will give you rest. . . . For My yoke is easy and My burden is light" (Matt. 11:28, 30).

The ministry, by nature, is a stressful occupation. Ministers go into the ministry because they care about people and they love seeing God change lives. A minister's greatest joy is seeing God change lives through the proclaiming of his Word. Most ministers enter into the ministry out of a desire to preach, teach, disciple, or evangelize. However, a minister quickly realizes that in addition to being a propagator of the gospel, he is also a CEO (with all the responsibilities but very few of the perks), an administrator, a mediator, a counselor, an educator, a public servant, a social activist, a chaplain, and more.

A pastor is quickly pulled in different and opposite directions. It seems people subconsciously expect ministers to model, lead, serve, fix, and cure the struggles that face their community, their church, and their family. If a pastor is going to last, he must learn how to manage the tension or stress that will result from these unrealistic expectations.

Pastors who have lasting ministries know how to set priorities—for themselves and the church. The following five essential priorities will help manage stress on a personal level:

Priority One—your relationship with God and your spouse. (As discussed in chapter 2, these two essential relationships are intertwined and cannot be separated.) Protecting priority one will involve:

- Guarding your prayer time and devotional life with God as an individual and as a couple.
- Keeping account of sins and offenses confessed, apologized for, and resolved between you and God as well as between you and your spouse.
- Communicating openly, honestly, and consistently with God and your spouse.
- Taking time to have fun with your spouse. Laugh and play together. If you can't laugh together, something is wrong. In the same way, take time to enjoy your relationship with the Father—treat him like someone you love.

(All of these things keep tension managed and shared in these relationships.)

Priority Two—protect your relationship with your children by refusing to allow church demands to steal you from them. The following are a few considerations to help maintain this delicate balance:

- ❏ They will have to learn how to share you; but "sharing" does not mean that they sacrifice their place of priority. If they feel they've lost you, they will resent God and the church.
- ❏ Open communication with your wife and accountability partners (lifeguards) can help judge how you are doing in this area.
- ❏ Your children will let you know as well, so listen to them. (Remember these are the *first and primary disciples* in your congregation.)
- ❏ Laugh with them. Play with them. No matter how old they are, they need to share some laughing time with you.

Priority Three—protect your relationship with yourself. Too often, it seems, ministers lose themselves in the ministry until there is nothing left of them. Then they become angry and resentful toward their families and their ministries as they burn out. They resent anyone who expects anything from them. Protecting your relationship with yourself involves the following:

- ❏ Protecting priorities one and two.
- ❏ Keeping some "quality" time for yourself, i.e. hobbies, time for relaxation, etc.
- ❏ Building habits that include proper diet and exercise.
- ❏ Scheduling, on a regular basis, getaways for yourself and immediate family. (Put them on the calendar; build them into your schedule like you do everything else.)
- ❏ Develop supportive friendships inside and outside the ministry.
- ❏ Set up your lifeguard system and keep it in place (accountability partners).

Priority Four—prioritize and lead your ministry. Do not allow it to lead you. People will let you know what they want, but you will have to discern what is needed. You decide how to share yourself and use your resources to meet those needs. Consider the following:

- ❏ Protect priorities one, two, and three. These three priorities will enable you to hear God and have the confidence to make hard decisions. (This is where vision comes from.)

- ❏ More needs than resources will always exist in the ministry. Your ability to hear God will enable you to have confidence in knowing when to say "yes" and when to say "no."

- ❏ When you know you've been obedient, weathering criticism becomes less stressful.

Priority Five—eliminate behaviors or choices that undermine priorities one through four. If seeking assistance is necessary to gain victory over the behaviors you are trying to eliminate, then that is what you must do.

"Let us lay aside every weight, and the sin which so easily ensnares us, and let us run with endurance the race that is set before us, looking unto Jesus, the author and finisher of our faith" (Heb. 12:1–2).

Appendix V

A Word to the Church

"Brethren, if a man is overtaken in any trespass, you who are spiritual restore such a one in a spirit of gentleness, considering yourself lest you also be tempted. Bear one another's burdens, and so fulfill the law of Christ" (Gal. 6:1–2).

All too often it seems churches are known more for "shooting their wounded" than their attempts to redeem them. This can especially be true when the fallen or wounded are among the ranks of church leadership. When churches are caught off guard by morally embarrassing situations, they tend to make rash, insensitive decisions. They want to make sure they do not appear to be endorsing or soft-peddling the fallen leaders' behavior. While it is important to stand for righteousness, it must not be done in a manner void of grace.

What message is being sent when ministers are let go with minimal assistance? The message is, "Don't get caught!" or "If you're tempted, there is nowhere to go for help." The result is that church leadership suffers in secrecy. Then, in their secrecy, they fall, because secrets equal sickness. The secret isolates and eliminates accountability, allowing the temptation process to proceed with no intervention.

Perhaps churches respond poorly because there is no plan, or the only plan is termination with a few gratuitous counseling sessions. What if part of a staff member's orientation to a new church included a legitimate plan for seeking assistance when dealing with an unhealthy marital situation or a prolonged struggle with temptation?

> Perhaps the churches respond poorly because there is no plan, or the only plan is termination with a few gratuitous counseling sessions.

Safe & Sound provides a way to organize policies and responses to those struggling with the temptation process. It would be wise to sit down with church leadership to devise a plan of intervention. The plan should include answers to the following questions:

- ❑ Who should leadership turn to when struggling with temptation?
- ❑ What authority figures are to be informed?
- ❑ What is the nature of confidentiality?
- ❑ How will the leader, his family, and anyone else involved be protected while being held accountable and being given support?
- ❑ What are the options for the leader and the church depending on how far the leader has allowed the situation to progress before seeking assistance?
- ❑ What process will be used to walk through the above steps?

The church obviously has much more latitude to be gracious earlier in the process than later. The church might organize its response around four types of scenarios:

1.   Leader seeks help when the compromising behavior is minimal (as described in phases 1–3 of the Temptation Process).

2.   Leader seeks help at phase 4 when there is obvious compromising behavior through the violation of marriage vows or Christian ethics at an emotional level (as described in phase 4 of the Temptation Process).

3.   Leader seeks help at phase 5 where there is a blatant disregard (physical and emotional) of marriage vows or Christian ethics (as described in phase 5 of the Temptation Process).

4.   Leader is exposed separately from his own volition (as described in phase 6 of the Temptation Process).

Suggested Reading

Arterburn, Steve, and Fred Stoeker with Mike Yorkey. *Every Man's Battle: Every Man's Guide to . . . Winning the War on Sexual Temptation One Victory at a Time.* Sisters, Ore.: Waterbrook Press, 2000.

Cloud, Henry, and John Townsend. *Boundaries: When to Say Yes, When to Say No, to Take Control of Your Life.* Grand Rapids: Zondervan Publishing House, 1992.

Gottman, John. *Why Marriages Succeed or Fail . . . and How You Can Make Yours Last.* New York: Fireside Publishers, 1994.

Gottman, John M., and Nan Silver. *The Seven Principles for Making Marriage Work: A Practical Guide from the Country's Foremost Relationship Expert.* New York: Three Rivers Press, 1999.

Harley, Willard F., Jr. *His Needs, Her Needs, Building an Affair-proof Marriage.* Grand Rapids: Fleming H. Revell, 1994.

Laaser Mark. *Faithful and True: Sexual Integrity in a Fallen World.* Grand Rapids: Zondervan Publishing, 1996.

Smalley, Gary and Deboray. *Winning Your Wife Back: Before It's Too Late.* Nashville: Thomas Nelson, Inc., 1999.

Smalley, Gary, and Greg Smalley. *Winning Your Husband Back: Before It's Too Late.* by Nashville: Thomas Nelson, Inc., 1999.

Stinnett, Nick and Nancy; and Joe and Alice Beam. *Fantastic Families.* West Monroe, La.: Howard Publishing House, 1999.